MANAGING CONSTRUCTION CONFLICT

R. BADEN HELLARD

MANAGING CONSTRUCTION CONFLICT

Longman
Scientific &
Technical

Longman Group UK Limited,
Longman House, Burnt Mill, Harlow,
Essex CM20 2JE, England
and Associated Companies throughout the world.

© Longman Group UK Limited 1988

First published 1988

British Library Cataloguing in Publication Data

Hellard, R. Baden
   Managing construction conflict.
   1. Construction industry — Law and
   legislation — England 2. Building —
   Contracts and specifications — England
   I. Title
   344.203'78624   KD1641
   ISBN 0-582-00350-4

Set in Linotron 202 10/12pt Century Schoolbook

Printed and Bound in Great Britain
at the Bath Press, Avon.

'So long as human nature is what it is there will always be disputes. And those disputes, whatever their character, must be resolved – if society is to exist in a civilised way – as quickly, as cheaply, and as satisfactorily as possible.'

Lord Justice Roskill, Alexander Lecture, 1978.

'Conflict resolution is probably the most important area for the future of mankind and the continued existence of the world. Is it good enough to have it served in inadequate manner?'

Dr Edward de Bono, *Conflicts*, Harrap, 1985.

CONTENTS

LIST OF FIGURES

All diagrams have been developed by the author or by Polycon Consultants except Fig. 1.1 which is based on original work by the author with Sir Roger Walters, first published in RIBA Journal, February 1960.

FOREWORD

Disputes are almost inevitable in the fulfilment of construction contracts and, with those of significant magnitude or time span, the propensity for dispute is greater. This can arise out of interpretations of the contract. It can arise out of changes in circumstances from those envisaged at the time that the contract was agreed. It can arise out of inaccurate judgements on which the contract was based leading to adverse consequences in the outcome.

The Author argues cogently the case for an arbitrator in such disputes and presents an equally powerful case for not leaving it to our legal process to produce the solution. He traces the development of our legal systems and arbitration procedures over the years, culminating in the important recognition that arbitration, agreed by both parties, has the full support of the law behind it.

In a generation when our greatest growth industry has been that of mass media, its developers have long recognised that one of the foibles of human nature is to be fascinated with conflict; most of us love to view a fight, especially if we are not directly involved in it. In many ways, the exposure to such conflict compounds the problems created by it because it forces the protagonists into rigid polarisation with consequent escalation of the difficulties and a declining probability of acceptable solution.

This book which argues forcefully and logically from a tenable premise is therefore a timely contribution to a subject which has grown in significance in recent years and will continue to do so in the future.

THE LORD PENNOCK OF NORTON

12th August 1987

R. B. H.

AUTHOR'S FOREWORD

Dispute resolution in civil technical disputes is too important to be left to the lawyers and the courts. It is for this reason that in many areas of commerce parties to a contract have stipulated that their commercial differences should rather be determined by arbitrators – who should be technical, rather than legal, experts.

Arbitration has developed internationally and expanded rapidly in the last thirty years and the role of the Arbitrator is recognised and supported by the law in well over 100 countries. The development of an international model law is being actively pursued under the aegis of the United Nations Committee on International Trade Law (UNCITRAL). Yet, many companies whose operations would benefit from third-party intervention refuse to consider the process because they are required to accept the Award as final and binding sometimes in advance of the Arbitrator's appointment and when his identity is unknown to them.

From a personal involvement as an Arbitrator since 1952 and as a management consultant for nearly as long I believe that parties in construction disputes require a philosophy, techniques and developed resources far closer to the practices of modern management within the framework of their own activities than to the courts and the law.

The parties can then involve themselves to a far greater extent in the management of, or the management out of, their own disputes than is customary 'when the lawyers are called in', whether the forum be a court of law or the more (allegedly) informal arbitration court room.

Undoubtedly, these management techniques will mostly require third-party intervention. Balance is required in all kinds of competitive human activity as is evidenced by the rulings of umpire, referee, touch judge, or Ombudsman.

Adjudication, that is the making of an Award over all matters disputed between the parties, will undoubtedly be required. But today these matters are mostly technical, certainly multi-disciplinary and complex in their cause, and conventional arbitration may be in need of further development.

Fair and just adjudication is more likely to result from an objective evaluation, after a depth study and analysis of the many factors by experts in the subject areas. If such experts are consciously retained by **both** parties and therefore owe their duty of care jointly to both parties the chances are further improved. If they then arrive at their conclusions as a collective judgment after adopting devil's advocate postures only when this seems necessary to arrive at the most likely for a range of possible facts, the probabilities of success are still further increased.

The adversarial principle of the English courts where two lawyers present a case, the technical aspects of which they have fought hard only to begin to understand, to a third, a judge, who must decide only on the evidence put before him in accordance with the court rules, does not improve the chances of a just and technically correct solution. Particularly will this be so after the judge, knowledgeable in and concerned only with applying the law to the evidence (or the evidence he has heard to the law) hears the technical evidence of experts for one side which appears to tell him one thing, only to be reversed by the technical evidence of equal experts appearing for the other side!

The real factors causing the dispute are often obscure or deliberately masked by the presentation of the lawyers for both parties. The purpose and professional duty of each is to get the best result for his client, precluding the judge from the opportunity of deciding anything but the law apparently most appropriate for the case. He does this from previous but different cases decided probably before the modern technology now involved was invented!

English arbitration has, since 1889 at any rate, permitted an Arbitrator to adopt within the limits of natural justice whatever procedures are necessary to arrive at his conclusions on the real technical cause and so to make an Award.

But today dispute resolution requires skills and experience ranging over the wide subject areas of technology from which the dispute developed. Knowledge of the 'customs of the trade' are also required to extend across the whole management spectrum as well as the technologies.

Dispute resolution therefore requires a well-managed adjudication team approach. 'The law', and therefore the knowledge of lawyers, and their skills in the customs and practice of the law must be given much lower significance.

I have tried to present these concepts in an analytical manner which, like the concept itself, is midway between the practice of management and the custom of the courts.

But my belief, and I hope my message, is clear. Contractual disputes in Construction arise out of situations where technical, logistic and building trade customs and practice are the matters at issue – not the law.

Such disputes, and others in many areas of twentieth-century technology, will be better decided by consciously developed 'management' practices suited to the arena of Construction than by the customs of the courts and the lawyers who practise there.

I have also tried to structure the book to assist readers who seek different guidance from it. For example, those who only want to know 'what to do' can safely skip Chapters 2 and 3 and to a lesser extent Chapter 4.

A more detailed map follows, and an analysis at the end of Chapter 1 will help each reader answer his own particular needs.

I hope I have succeeded.

R. B. H.

ACKNOWLEDGEMENTS

Acknowledged in the body of the text are those whose words I have quoted specifically. But this book represents experience gained from practice over thirty years in the fields of projects, management and arbitration.

It therefore owes a great deal to those clients, colleagues, collaborators, contractors, disputants and others whose situations and ideas have stimulated the thought processes without which the book could not have been written.

Acknowledgements are therefore due to the many whose projects, assignments and ideas both successful and otherwise have contributed to my theme. I hope that those whose words I may over the years have taken as my own will forgive me for not having identified them.

But I am conscious that some of my colleagues past and present such as John Cane, Jim Connolly, Cedric Barclay, Clifford Clark, Herbert Cruikshank, Woodbine Parish, Jim Nisbet, Wilfrid Cantwell, Noel Mulcahy and others from whom I have learnt a great deal may recognise within the text thoughts which they initiated but which I have developed in ways for which, unless they wish, I do not hold them responsible, but for which I am nevertheless grateful.

I am also grateful to Diana Porter who has patiently recorded much of the material from which this manuscript has finally emerged.

To all of those, my sincere thanks.

The Author and the Publishers are also grateful to:

The British Property Federation
The Chartered Institute of Arbitrators
(and the Association of British Travel Agents)
The Royal Institute of British Architects
The Royal Institution of Chartered Surveyors

for their permission to reproduce in Chapter 6 and in Appendix I Arbitration Appointment Forms and Procedures which are their copyright;

and also to:

Peter Moro, CBE for permission to reproduce documents prepared for him by the Author.

We are also indebted to the following for permission to reproduce copyright material:

Elseviér Science Publishing Co., Inc. for fig. 4.4 from 'A Preface to Motivation Theory' by A. H. Maslow in *Psychosomatic Medicine*, Vol. 5, Copyright 1943 by The American Psychosomatic Society, Inc.

DEFINITIONS OF DISPUTE RESOLUTION PROCEDURES

Litigation
The process of contesting a dispute by a civil action in a court of law. This can arise either from a contract between the parties or can be an action in tort; that is a claim for damages over a private or civil wrong.

Arbitration
The handing down of an Award enforceable at law as the settlement of a dispute arising either from a contract in which an arbitration clause was included or as the result of a joint agreement to refer matters in difference to a third party appointed by or on behalf of the parties. The Arbitration Acts 1950 and 1979 define the powers of the Arbitrator under section 12(I) of the Act:

> ... the parties ... shall ... submit to be examined **by the Arbitrator or Umpire** ... and shall ... produce **before the Arbitrator or Umpire** all documents within their possession or power respectively which may be **required or called for**, and do all other things which during the proceedings on the reference **the Arbitrator or Umpire may require**.

The parties in entering arbitration are bound to accept the Arbitration Award as final and binding upon them and the Award is as enforceable as a judgment of the court.

Adjudication
The process of making an Award by a procedure similar to arbitration but the parties are not bound at the time of making the appointment to accept the Adjudicator's Award as final and binding and have a given time after its publication to do so.

Conciliation*
Interposing a third party who has not been involved between the two parties to a dispute or difference, to clarify the issues between them.

Mediation*
The taking of active steps by a third party making suggestions to both sides to try to find a solution acceptable to both sides.

---

*Neither mediation nor conciliation involve the handing down of an award.

Conflict

The opposition of interests, values or objectives.

Confliction

A word created and defined by Edward de Bono as the process of setting up, promoting or encouraging conflict. It is the deliberate effort put into creating a conflict.

De-confliction

The opposite of confliction. Designing away or dissipating the basis of conflict. The effort required to evaporate a conflict.

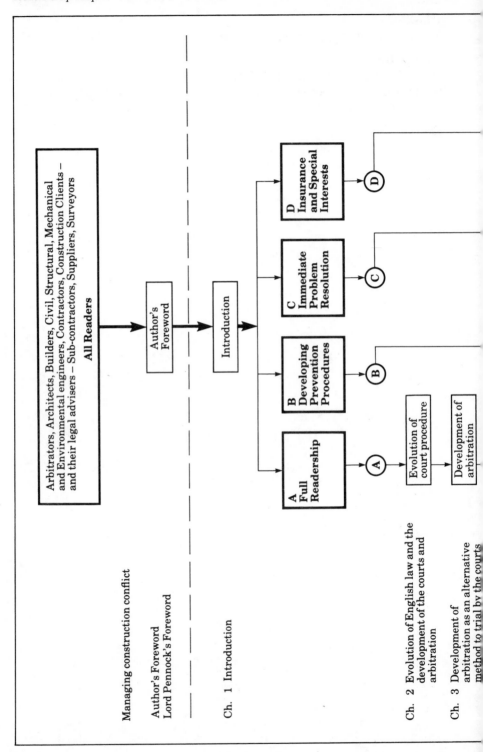

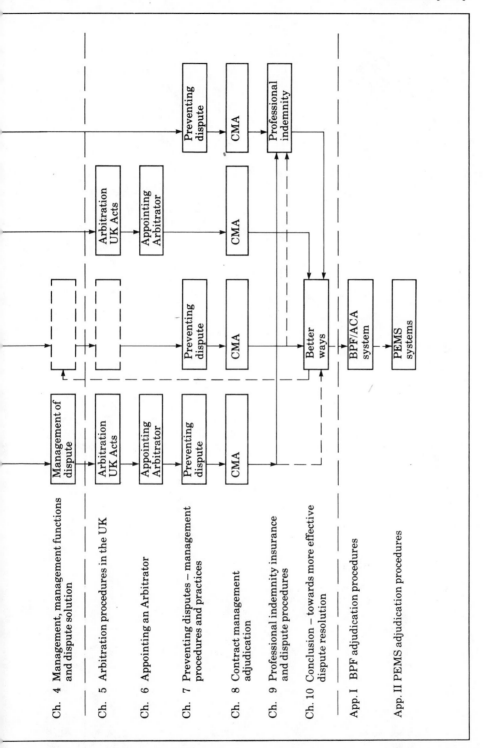

Ch. 4 Management, management functions and dispute solution

Ch. 5 Arbitration procedures in the UK

Ch. 6 Appointing an Arbitrator

Ch. 7 Preventing disputes – management procedures and practices

Ch. 8 Contract management adjudication

Ch. 9 Professional indemnity insurance and dispute procedures

Ch. 10 Conclusion – towards more effective dispute resolution

App. I BPF adjudication procedures

App. II PEMS adjudication procedures

PART I

THE EVOLUTIONARY BACKGROUND TO CONSTRUCTION DISPUTE

CHAPTER 1

INTRODUCTION

*The organisation of the Construction Industry today is
a built-in recipe for conflict.*

*Each group of professionals, contractors and
subcontractors have developed customs and practices
which frequently continue when the building 'team'
carries out what is a combined operation for
essentially prototype constructions. Frequently the
building owner is the only 'non-expert' in the team and
it is he who has to make the key project decisions.*

*It is this background that led to Construction being
one of the leaders in the development of arbitration as
an alternative to the courts in resolving disputes
arising from unique construction contracts.*

*But many are as dissatisfied with arbitration as
with litigation and require a quicker, cheaper and
better way of resolving disputes if they cannot prevent
them arising.*

*Disputes arise between men even if they result from
problems with materials, machines, methods and
money – the resources of management. The use of
management techniques arising from a study of
management principles and practices are more likely
to be conducive to a satisfactory resolution of such
disputes than the practice of the courts – but they
should embrace some of the excellent concepts of
arbitration.*

This book is about the resolution of disputes in the Construction Industry. It is principally concerned with better methods of resolving technical and commercial, that is contractual, disputes but within the
context of the law.

3

But it is not a legal textbook nor is it for reference by non-legal professionals or parties. Too many of those exist already and too many disputants attempt to resolve their problems by recourse to the courts, or to formal arbitration – to quote Sir John Donaldson when both Master of the Rolls **and** President of the Chartered Institute of Arbitrators – 'its private sector handmaiden'.

As far as the Construction Industry is concerned, arbitration emerged as a sensible alternative to the courts at the beginning of the century because those involved in it realised that there were many technical causes of dispute that were not understood by lawyers and perhaps because a private forum was the better place to discuss these matters before a judge who understood them and was himself generally involved in them in his day-to-day activities.

Certainly, Construction was fully represented by the founders of the Institute of Arbitrators in 1915 who were an architect, an engineer, a secretary, an accountant and two solicitors, with the eminent Lord Headley its first President.

To understand why this should be so and why Construction, along with Charter-parties in the Shipping Industry, was one of the three areas where arbitration developed in the UK, let me examine the evolution of the Construction Industry and the development of the various parties involved in a modern construction project and the nature of their relationships.

Project management relationships

Initially the relationship between the builder and the client, or group requiring the building, was simple (see Fig. 1.1).

These customary practices and the relationships between the different groups have been further complicated by the organisational or contractual groupings of the different functional elements. Multi-disciplinary professional firms, sometimes combine with general building contractors to carry out specific projects as joint ventures, whilst the combination of specialist suppliers and subcontractors with, or as off-shoots from, larger main contractors are probably now the norm on any large project.

The ultimate in this situation has probably been reached on projects like the Channel Tunnel where several general contracting firms in the UK and in France combined with several banks to become two entrepreneurial companies, indivisibly linked by dividing each share into half held in each other's company.

This parent company then placed contracts with the various contracting companies who were major shareholders for the construction of the

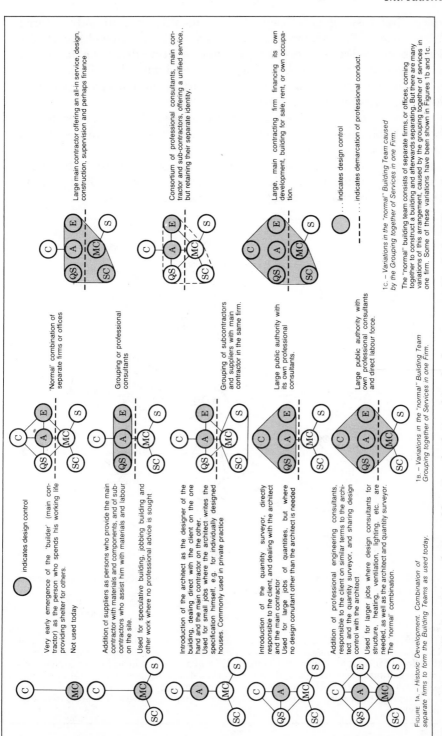

Fig. 1.1 (a)–(c) The historic evolution of functional relationships for firms engaged in the building industry and their operational groupings (based upon work by Sir Roger T Walters. RIBA Journal, Feb. 1960).

project, but these general contracting companies had already entered into a variety of arrangements with dozens of firms, some of them their own subsidiaries and others professional consulting firms, for the design and supply of components or services connected with the project.

But these complexities are still only part of the pattern of relationships that are created on a project.

Others are formed through the constraints or influences of people and organisations outside 'the client' and the team assembled to design and construct his requirements.

Figure 1.2 identifies those external to the project team with whom the building owner, his architect or project manager must first come to terms to ensure that the client's requirements can be met.

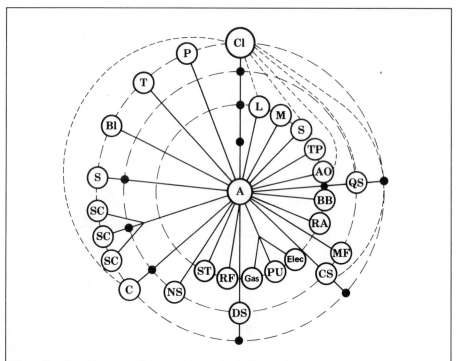

Note: Rough guidance on time is given by the distance of the out stations from the centre. The earlier contacts are nearer the centre.

Group 1: Cl – client; L – landlord, leaseholders; M – ministries; S – solicitors; TP – town planning authority; AO – adjoining owners; BB – building by law authority; RA – research associations; PU – public utility undertakings – gas, electricity, water; RF – Royal Fine Art Commission. **Group 2:** QS – quantity surveyor; MF – manufacturers; CS – consultants – Services and Structural; DS – designing specialist; NS – nominated specialists and suppliers. **Group 3:** C – main contractor; SC – subcontractors; S – suppliers; Bl – Building Inspectors – district surveyors; T – tenants, lessees; P – press (technical and lay).

Fig. 1.2 The organisation network for a building project.

Getting the brief

Every construction project has four frequently conflicting elements which must be established in 'the brief'. These four can be classified by the code word FACT.

- **Function** – all the technical and physical requirements: space, servicing, internal relationship between the parts, access, egress and the like.
- **Aesthetic** – that is, the satisfaction of all the human and subjective aspects that will be enshrined in the end result. The modern equivalent of commodity firmness and delight. But today there are always requirements as to:
- **Cost** – both capital and running costs. Perhaps better expressed as lifetime cost of the project.
- **Time** – the logistic requirements for commercial completion and occupation which in some cases, for example a short-term exhibition project, can be the most critical requirement in the client's brief.

Sometimes the requirements under each of these headings can, or should be, provided by the client but sometimes they must be established from the person or authority that can exercise a modifying or even controlling influence over the matter. The influence of such external authorities is rarely complete or a matter of black and white. Even when the control, such as with town planning authorities, has statutory power, negotiation can still result in satisfactory solutions to seemingly impossible conflicts in requirements.

In these situations the client's representative, project manager or design team leader, to use the recent terminology established by the British Property Federation's (BPF) *System of Organisation for Building Projects*, can still bring about a satisfactory solution by negotiation, and the design may be the better for the challenge presented by these conflicting requirements.

However, it can clearly be seen that when so many people are involved in providing the criteria for the brief and so many technologies are involved in satisfying the requirements of the brief in a design solution, even before work begins on site, the whole situation is one where conflict of requirements' and in the resources available to satisfy the requirements' abound.

If we give all those involved the credit of wishing to perform their own tasks to the best of their ability then it can easily be seen that there is the need for a great deal of negotiation, which in its turn will demand excellent communication ability by the person or persons responsible for finalising the design brief.

Many of these negotiations will continue over weeks or months and be interactive as between the client's stated requirements and the constraints imposed by the external parties, many of which will themselves be in conflict with each other.

At some point the design must be frozen to enable the second stage of the operation – the detailing of materials with their consequent quality and cost implications – so that a tender can be obtained for implementing the design by construction.

The degree of finality in the price obtained from the various contractors for the work required of them will, or should, depend upon the extent of the firmness of the requirements stated in the tender. The greater the firmness the less the contractor's risk. Therefore the more competitive should be the price.

But whatever the contract obtained in terms of time and price, the external constraints, if not the client's own situation, are subject to the possibility of continuing change. The people or controlling power within the external authority can result in changes of policy, and these in turn can produce a different situation which might be to the building owner's disadvantage, or might produce a relaxation from which the building owner can benefit and so produce changes to the brief or design requirements, which in turn can change design and so reflect upon the contractual terms.

All this is perhaps to state the obvious, and shows why building contracts provide for variations within the contract. But, in principle, every change does create a situation where the cost and time criteria are completely open to renegotiation. The various standard forms of contract have grown in size to prescribe what are essentially 'customs and practices' for dealing with this situation, and being customs and practices which are developed and indeed argued over within the Industry, they reflect more the conditions generally felt to be prevailing within the Industry than they do the legal environment outside the Industry. Yet, when disputes are taken to the courts the criteria used for their progress and resolution are those of the law and the lawyers rather than those of the parties to the construction project.

Thus, arbitration, the resolution of disputes arising out of the project by a technical Arbitrator drawn from amongst the ranks of those regularly involved in construction projects, developed as a better way of resolving the dispute. But in the last decade there has been growing dissatisfaction with the arbitration concept and more particularly of the outcome of many cases put through the arbitration procedures.

There has been a substantial increase in the time spent and the costs incurred in going to arbitration. This has led many parties to the view that arbitration is at least no less expensive than the courts. Sometimes too the Arbitration Tribunal is not much better fitted to resolve the case than the courts, and finally the appeals procedures that have applied to arbitration in the UK mean that the principle of the Arbitrator's Award being final and binding can be thwarted by one party later appealing to the courts with consequent overall delay and even more cost.

The practice of arbitration and that of arbitrators has, during this last decade or so, been substantially improved through the development of training systems and of arbitration procedures by the Institute, now Chartered Institute, of Arbitrators. Knowledge of the law by technical arbitrators has been developed through these training courses and the cadre of arbitrators has been strengthened by the recruitment of senior professionals in many disciplines, and in particular by the addition of lawyer arbitrators coming from the Bench, the Bar and the Law Society.

Unfortunately, this has also had the effect of moving arbitration and the approach by many arbitrators away from the technical factors and the customs and practices of the Industry and towards the customs and practices of the law.

At the same time Construction has become ever-more complex and technical and the relationships and contractual groupings of those involved in the approach are also more complex and contractually varied.

Even the parties to a project entered into with a form of contract which contains provision for arbitration – the arbitration clause – are loath to use it, whilst others are loath to enter into a contract that contains an arbitration clause. We must therefore look for yet better ways of resolving the disputes that will inevitably arise in projects such as Construction which are one-off, generally of a prototype nature, and where satisfaction must be sought in relation to the particular project rather than through a series of continuing or continuous relationships.

Conciliation, the intervention of a third party to bring together those in conflict, and mediation, a similar function, but one where the third party himself makes suggestions as to the terms of the settlement, are approaches which have been used to bring about a cooling between parties in heated conflict, particularly between management and workers in industrial relations situations. But those disputes are of a simpler nature than those found in Construction. Neither technique is intended to imply a binding result upon the parties, and finality is sought as an essential element in dispute resolution.

Where then can we look to assist in this reappraisal and review? Where are we likely to find other principles of scientific or philosophic development that can be applied to the resolution of disputes, or to their prevention?

Modern scientific principles of management have themselves emerged in the twentieth century from the initial studies of Taylor and Gilbreth at the end of the nineteenth century. Both were possessed of the conviction that 'there is always a better way' and that the study of work done would highlight the direction of this better way.

Management is about balance. The balance of requirements against resources, of income against expenditure, and of the often conflicting needs between the achievement of collective or corporate goals with those of the individuals involved in their overall achievement.

Management is also about maintaining the balance between the law on the one hand, and custom and practice on the other, whilst moving dynamically through the direction of resources, human and others, to achieve a given objective.

It is therefore concerned with men, machines, materials, methods, money and *motivation*.

It is from within these matters that disputes arise. It is therefore likely that the resolution of these disputes will also be better found within them than by moving out to resolve matters in the extraneous, and generally irrelevant to the cause, arena of the courts. Here the lawyers are the skilled and it is their customs and practices alone which prevail.

Examination of management philosophies, functions and practices confirms the practicality of this thesis.

I shall examine in turn in the succeeding chapters the evolution, strengths and weaknesses of the UK procedures and practices of the courts, of arbitration, the customs and practices of the construction process and its industrial structure and then put forward practical proposals for the prevention of dispute and for better methods of constraining and resolving them.

These new methods embrace both adjudication by third-party intervention and techniques to reduce the development of conflict. Both are very relevant to the management (and resolution) of dispute which will in turn have a substantial influence on the productivity and therefore profitability for those who undertake building projects, whether as client, consultant or contractor.

The reader who requires to know only what he should do to prevent disputes arising can safely skip Chapters 2 and 3 and perhaps the whole of Part II without loss of necessary information, but all will benefit, and maintain full continuity, if they also read the synopsis which precedes each chapter. Those who already have a dispute will find Chapters 5, 6, 8 and 10 of particular relevance, and may only wish to return to Chapters 4 and 7 to prevent a recurrence in their future operations.

The serious professional who has a duty to advise his client on either prevention or cure will find analysis and reasoned argument in Chapters 2, 3 and 4 to support the recommendations made in Chapters 7 and 8, and in Chapter 9 those same professionals should find some help in reducing the risk and costs of their own frailty in relation to their professional indemnity protection.

Rather, it is concerned with evaluating these two conventional methods of resolving disputes in the context of a complex, fast-moving and technological Construction Industry, and then proposing practical methods better fitted to the arena of Construction from which the particular differences have arisen. By extracting the best approaches from a variety of other areas we arrive at a logical, effective and economic approach that will be far more acceptable to those unfortunate parties who find themselves in conflict over a building or construction project.

This is therefore essentially a management book. A book concerned with better ways of resolving conflict and the dispute situation, and so returning the parties to normal and productive relations.

Events create situations but disputes arise between people. People whose purpose, procedures and practices which were theoretically in balance when the contract – the description of their legally binding promises – was made and who now find themselves with conflicts of interest that cannot be resolved between them after something unforeseen has occurred on the project.

In the distant past, when such civil disputes occurred, the only course open to the parties was to the courts. There bewigged counsel, like the champions of old, fight again, but now armed only with the more civilised eloquence of words and their knowledge of previous verbal battles that had won the day in similar verbal duels. But the courts provide a context far removed from the factual cause and the technical, cultural and possibly social arena of the dispute. In court the dispute is referred to the judgment of one learned solely in the law, and on grounds of legal argument familiar only to the jousters and the judge.

The Construction Industry exists on the one hand within the framework of law but also by a balance maintained on the other with what can be called 'custom and practice'.

Every culture, society, club, trade union, profession and social group develops customs and rules, written and unwritten, which govern its actions, probably more than the regulations under which it was set up or continues to exist.

Within the Construction Industry, architects, quantity surveyors, engineers, contractors and various specialists, all have, in addition to their special technical skills, their own trade or professional customs and practice, some of which come together in an overall framework for building projects, but some of which do not.

Changes happen slowly, particularly in the older cultures, such as the law, but today the pace of change outside that culture at least merits a more frequent – and perhaps continuous – review.

Change is generally mooted only when the old pattern can clearly be seen, both within as well as without the established group, to be essential to the continued well-being of that group, and in a manner acceptable to those within it, particularly when the pressure is from outside. Lawyers, both on the Bench (and in the Court of Appeal), at the Bar, and within the ranks of the solicitors, are now re-examining these practices to improve their acceptability to those who, perforce, must or want to use them. But, at the latter end of the twentieth century construction disputes need a completely different alternative.

'Arbitration', a procedure recognised as an alternative – and supported by the courts as a better way for some commercial disputes –

emerged at the end of the nineteenth century and has been of great benefit and provided a successful alternative internationally in the twentieth. Particularly is this so where the arena for the hearing of the dispute and the experience of the Arbitrator who makes the Award mirrors that of the parties and is close to the subject-matter causing the difference. But perhaps it too, after approximately 100 years of development, now needs fundamental reappraisal, or maybe to return closer to first principles.

Those arbitrators and experts practising regularly in the arena of dispute resolution will, I hope, be persuaded that the complete work provides all the history, logic and emotional thrust of argument that will help in the further evolution of better ways to serve their clients and so reduce the time, cost and traumatic experience in resolving the disputes which will sometimes arise no matter how good the project management.

CHAPTER 2

THE EVOLUTION OF ENGLISH LAW AND THE DEVELOPMENT OF THE COURTS AND ARBITRATION

The Medieval origins of the courts as a means of resolving civil disputes. Trial by oath or ordeal, and after 1066 trial by battle – all reflect the concept of trial by the supernatural. The concept of jurors – oath swearers – who originally supported a litigant but later became the twelve 'local experts' who would have the knowledge of local customs to decide on matters at issue, before the judge who presided over the court, made his award.

*Trial by jury evolved with the jury taking outside evidence to supplement their own local knowledge until eventually a trial became based **only** on the evidence submitted to the jury. Only in the nineteenth century did trial by a single judge become the norm when, in 1895 the Commercial Court was set up where the judges alone decided – even then judges sought reference from expert witnesses.*

Not until 1919 was right to trial by jury withdrawn except in cases of turpitude and in 1933 the grand jury was abolished save for fraud, libel, slander, etc.

The current framework of the courts under the 1981 Supreme Court Act is illustrated with appeal routes.

In Anglo-Saxon times trial was by oath or ordeal. Where parties were in dispute the court would decide who should be put to the test to prove their case. The parties then chose whether to elect for the trial by oath or ordeal.

Ordeal was by hot iron or hot ploughshare. If you emerged unscathed from grasping the hot iron or walking hot foot over the ploughshare

13

then you won. This method was abolished by the Lateran Council in 1215.

Alternatively, if the trial was by oath you, and usually twelve oath-helpers, had to take the same or a similar oath. Pollock and Maitland's *History of English Law* gives a vivid picture of litigants arriving at court each accompanied by his suit of witnesses, each ready to perform the swearing should proof be awarded against him. 'A punctilious regard for formalities is required of the swearers. If a wrong word is used the oath "bursts" and the adversary wins. In the twelfth century such elaborate forms of asseveration had been devised that, rather than attempt them, men would take their chance at the hot iron.'

The Normans arriving in England brought with them the concept of trial by battle. This not only dealt with proof but it was also a direct trial between the parties. Perhaps a bilateral ordeal.

It was also a method bound with elaborate rules. A space 60 feet square was laid out and a pavilion set up at one side for the bench and a bar for the lawyers. In a civil case the parties might be, and I presume usually were, represented by champions. There was a regular trade of professional pugilists for the purpose. They were armed with batons; they wore armour but their arms, heads and legs were bare. They were required to take an oath against witchcraft: Blackstone gives its terms as follows: 'Here this, ye justices, that I have this day neither eat nor drank nor have upon me neither bone stone nor grass nor any enchantment sorcery or witchcraft whereby the law of God may be abased or the law of the devil exalted, so help me God.' At dawn the combatants were required to fight until one was vanquished. If they were still fighting at nightfall the one on whom lay the burden of proof had lost. The last trial by battle seems to have taken place in Westminster in 1571.

All of these methods owed something to the supernatural (or to superstition?). Men were unwilling to take upon themselves the task of judging where lay the truth. That was a matter for God and he was seen to preside over the ordeal or the oath and the outcome of battle.

Development of trial by jury

In the twelfth century Henry II was a great lawgiver and trial by jury was developing. The word 'jurer' simply meant a person who takes an oath and a jury is thus a number of persons who have done so. The first jury was purely an administrative device. When information was needed by the Norman kings they sought answers from local men who were supposed to know the facts and were put on oath to provide the answers. This was how the Domesday Book was developed.

Henry II ordained that in a dispute about ownership of land a litigant might obtain a royal writ to have a jury summoned to decide the matter. Jurors were drawn from men in the neighbourhood who were taken to have knowledge of all the relevant facts and anyone who was ignorant was rejected from service on the jury.

These men were bound to answer upon their oath and according to their knowledge of the facts. When a party got twelve oaths in his favour he won. Hence the origins of the jury trial which was then extended beyond land disputes into other matters and so began a gradual process whereby the character of the jury of twelve men changed. First they were allowed to supplement their own local knowledge by information received from outside until eventually a jury became en-titled to act only upon information from outside formally given as evidence in court.

By the Stuart times the jury had become judges of both civil and criminal matters. It was they and not the judge who presided at the trial that decided the questions of fact in civil cases. This jury system, a peculiarly English institution, has been exported overseas with our common law and has even been instituted in some Continental systems. In England it eventually ousted the earlier modes of trial and reigned supreme in the courts until 1933 when the grand jury was abolished excepting for libel, slander, malicious prosecution, false imprisonment, seduction and breach of promise in marriage.

Whilst the last recorded trial by battle took place in Tothill Fields in 1571 the procedure was not abolished by law until 1818.

This repeal came about following the case of *Ashford* v. *Thornton* in 1817. An appeal of felony was brought against Abraham Thornton, who had been acquitted of the murder of Mary Ashford. Mary Ashford had died on the way home from a dance in the village of Erdington near Birmingham. A number of influential people thought there had been a miscarriage of justice and invoked the antique procedure of appeal of felony. This allowed the next of kin to sue the alleged felon in a civil action. William Ashford, the dead girl's brother, a small and timid man, was the plaintiff. Thornton's lawyers found that a trial by battle could be demanded, and when Thornton was arraigned he threw down the gauntlet and demanded battle. Ashford declined the combat and the case collapsed. The following year Parliament abolished trial by battle – and also the appeal of felony.

Development of the law

Having considered the evolution of the methods of trial let us now look at the evolution of the law, the rules within which we are all expected to behave and against which standards the judges will measure and decide.

At the time of Henry II the courts comprised local lords and county sheriffs, earls and bishops in the shires and hundreds. There was also a *curia regis* – central royal court – but this was not open to all. Civil law was conducted by an 'assize of navel disseisin' which was initially concerned with land wrongly seized.

There was an attempt to develop uniform justice at this central court at Westminster, which court was closed while the judges went on circuit. By selecting the best rulings from current judgments a common law developed. This was essentially local customary law, a common law, but it was in fact 'created' by judges. This they justified as being based on local customs. Many of the itinerant judges were clerics, who could read and write, and they also were provided with a living by the Church, which was rich while the Crown was poor.

When these judges were not on circuit they sat in Westminster and established *stare decisis* which was judicial precedent, by which judges were to be bound and not just consider these earlier judgments as for their guidance. There has thus grown up on the one hand local law, equity and increasingly, statute law and foreign law, whilst on the other hand there is the common law of judicial precedent but which is really judge-made law.

In 1530 Sir Thomas Moore said if common law and equity were in conflict equity should prevail, and this has carried through into the Supreme Court Act of 1981. But, whilst equity never says common law is wrong it provides alternative solutions.

'Equity', the judicial precedents and a separate system before 1873, was then intended to soften the common law. Although it can be seen as 'fair play', to lawyers it means primarily the system of rules administered by Court of Chancery before the 1873/75 Judication Acts. It had its origins in medieval appeals made to the Lord Chancellor who was both the King's Chief Secretary and his Chaplain (or Keeper of the King's Conscience). As a priest he tended to decide on morality or natural justice (i.e. equity) rather than on the narrow technical rules of law.

Parliament-made law

In the fourteenth century Parliamentary legislation became more general and during the Tudor period statute law developed, and now in the twentieth century the bulk of statute law is large but still forms a comparatively small part of law as a whole – seen by lawyers as merely a set of disjointed rules. Yet, a statute – that is a law passed by Parliament – can do anything except change a man to a woman (although in a legal sense even this can be done). No court can question the validity of an Act of Parliament. A statute can abolish common law rules to cope with changing circumstances. However, any statute has to be repealed by Parliament and until its repeal it is absolutely binding. But Parliament cannot bind its successors and this has produced a constitutional conflict. For when Britain joined the European Economic Community the Community placed an obligation on member states to ensure that Community law is paramount.

The passing of a statute, or its repeal, by Parliament is the result of an interactive process between the House of Commons and the House of Lords. Ideals and purpose, frequently motivated by conflicting political attitudes and compromise within the House of Commons as well as differences with the House of Lords, may well result in a conflict of objectives which the courts will have to interpret later against specific cases put before them.

It is the judges, some of whom also sit in the House of Lords, who are responsible for interpreting in their courts the meaning of the statutes that emerge from Parliament. They also have to equate the meaning of the statutes which form the comparatively small part of the law as a whole with the body of common law (judge-made law) and judicial precedent.

The law merchant

The other facets which have had their implications on the general body of common law came from mercantile customs – *lex mercatoria*. The Court of Admiralty took over the rules of the law merchants and recognised merchant customs without requiring proof. This in turn has led to agreements being regarded as just as binding as contracts and becoming part of common law. For example, the Bills of Exchange Act of 1882, and more recently the Sale of Goods Act 1979.

Canon and Roman law

Other strains within the body of common law owe much to Roman law and canon law, which has had considerable emphasis, as one might expect, in most matrimonial and divorce cases, although there has also been much squabbling between lay and ecclesiastical members of the court over these matters and also those of probate.

Modern structure of the courts

In 1873 the court structure was revised with the High Court comprising five divisions:

- Queen's Bench;
- Common Pleas;
- Exchequer;
- Chancery;
- Admiralty, Probate and Divorce.

In 1881 this was consolidated into three divisions:

1. Queen's Bench (incorporating Common Pleas and the Exchequer Division).
2. Chancery.
3. Admiralty, Probate and Divorce.

In addition, there are the Court of Appeal and the House of Lords as higher courts for the hearing of appeals.

The most recent revision of the court structure was the Supreme Court Act of 1981, which established the House of Lords, and the Court of Appeal of the High Court, comprising:

(a) Chancery Division with twelve puisne (pronounced puny) judges with the Lord Chancellor as President, and with a Company Court. The Chancery Division deals with mortgages, trusts, revenue matters, deeds and documents, estates and contentious probate.

(b) The Queen's Bench Division, where all types of civil law action can be brought, particularly contractual and tortious matters.

The Commercial Court and the Official Receiver's Courts are also part of Queen's Bench. The Division has forty judges presided over by the Lord Chief Justice. This Act also permits judges to sit as arbitrators which hearings can be in private.

(c) The Family Division, where seventeen judges deal with divorce, custody of children and non-contentious probate.

(d) There is also a Restrictive Practices Court.

(e) Over all sits the Court of Appeal where eighteen Lord Justices plus the Lord Chancellor, the Lord Chief Justice, the President of the Family Division and ex-Lord Chancellors and ex-Law Lords sit to oversee the judgments of the courts of first instance.

The Court of Appeal sits as a tribunal of three to hear appeals from the lower courts.

(f) Further appeal can be made from the Court of Appeal to the House of Lords which used to be the end of the matter. But now that Britain is a member of the EEC appeals can also be made to the **European Court of Justice** in Luxemburg whose judgments must be accepted by member states. This court works substantially on

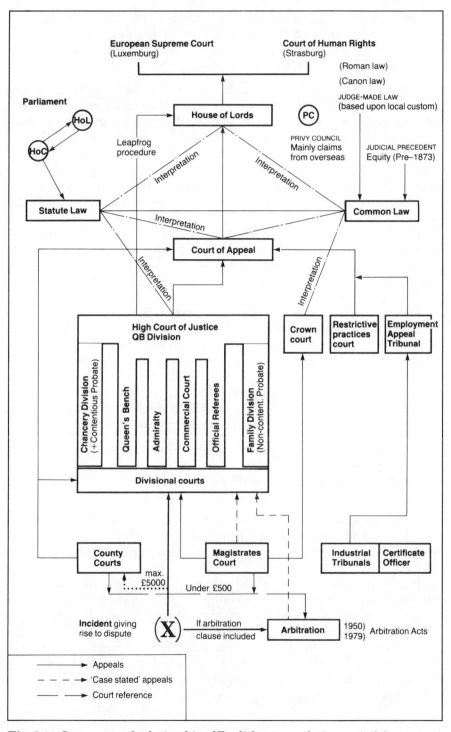

Fig. 2.1 Structure and relationship of English courts relating to civil disputes.

written submissions and seeks to interpret the Treaty of Rome in relation to the matter at issue. The court has one judge from each member state, all thirteen of whom sit to consider any case put before it. It can and does act inquisitorially.

The European Court rules on such matters as the interpretation and enforcement of EEC regulations affecting all member states. For example, that the working hours of long-distance commercial drivers should be regulated and that a tachograph should be installed in the cab of each vehicle to monitor the driver's compliance with the regulations. This matter was one in which Britain, due to pressure from the trade unions, delayed introducing legislation until it was eventually forced by the European Court to do so, despite the continued opposition from the Transport and General Workers' Union.

The European Court of Human Rights which sits in Strasburg considers matters of individual rights and fundamental freedoms. It was this court that was responsible recently for decreeing that men and women should have equal rights over the age at which they should be forced to retire from work.

A female nursing sister who had been retired at the age of 60 complained to the court that whilst she had been forced to retire at the age of 60 a male equivalent could continue until he was 65 years old before being forced to retire. The court found that this was a sexual inequality which should not be permitted. As a consequence every organisation, large or small, within Britain has had to review its age structure for retirement, with tremendous consequences on pension schemes, insurance matters and the like. The options for each firm were clearly:

(a) to allow men to retire at 60; or
(b) to allow women to retire at 65; or,
(c) give both the option of either.

All of these options had substantial implications and repercussions on the terms and conditions of engagement and many other contracts which had been entered into between employer and long-term employees many years earlier.

Figure 2.1 illustrates this current structure and the flow of appeals that exist and through which a civil dispute progresses. It can be seen that finality can be a long way off even at the end of a long trial in a court of first instance! An awesome thought for would-be litigants. This illustrates why it is said that a civil action in the courts is only for the very rich – or for the very poor who, providing they have less than £4700 disposable assets can obtain legal aid for a civil action.

Undoubtedly litigation is for the lawyers.

CHAPTER 3

THE DEVELOPMENT OF ARBITRATION AS AN ALTERNATIVE METHOD TO TRIAL BY THE COURTS

Roman origins of the Arbitrator, the need for quicker settlement of merchants' disputes as trade developed in the Middle Ages. The trend for trial by judge not jury.

The stimulus of the Industrial Revolution for technical arbitration.

The supervision of arbitration by the courts – the 'case stated' and its abuse, the benefits of arbitration and its essential characteristics and advantages over litigation for technical matters.

So much for the medieval background to the English courts.

What has led to the concept of arbitration – outside the courts? And now for the conduct of small claims by arbitration within them?

Perhaps the Roman Republic is the first realistic starting-point for the evolution of methods of dispute settlement outside of the strictly legal system.

In 280 BC the principal magistrate was the praetor who for one year presided over litigation. He was not necessarily a lawyer and none of his 'judgments' bound his successors. His role was to decide issues disputed between citizens of Rome, and later a second **praetor perigrinus** took charge of cases where a foreigner was concerned.

Trade was developing and so a code of rules – not Roman civil law – but the law of nations, **ius gentium**, was used for these trading disputes.

In the Middle Ages merchants travelling around Europe needed quicker settlement of their disputes and within the customs and practices of their own calling. In Britain in 1478, sitting in the Star Chamber in the Palace of Westminster where the Privy Council tried both civil and criminal cases, especially those affecting the Crown's interests, the Chancellor said:

'This dispute is brought by an alien merchant who has come to conduct his case here, and he ought not to be held to await trial by twelve men and other solemnities of the law of the land but ought to be able to sue here from hour to hour and day to day for the speed of merchants.' (The court was abolished in 1640 as its judgments were thought to be too arbitrary.)

It had been recognised that for a century or more such cases had been decided by 'the law merchant' where in England it was administered in the Pie Powder Court – *pieds poudres* – the Court of Dusty Feet.

In the fourteenth century the law merchant was beginning to be absorbed into the royal courts, where speed, simplicity of procedure and privacy were emphasised.

But by the seventeenth century the local courts had become antiquated, cumbersome in procedure and ineffectual, and so not surprisingly, and perhaps like today, highly unpopular.

Arbitration – the trial of a civil matter by a single person rather than by a jury – was established before 1800 but grew rapidly with the Industrial Revolution. It provided the courts – and the common law – with both a challenge and an example, and by the mid-nineteenth century Parliament had been pushed partly by arbitration practice to make the judges deciders of fact as well as law. This love-hate relationship between lawyers and arbitrators has continued ever since.

In 1845, for example, the whole question of compensation for compulsory purchase of land was handed over to arbitrators in the Land Clauses Consolidation Act.

In 1854 the Common Law Procedure Act permitted a judge to refer an issue of fact to an Arbitrator to try, and in 1873 the Judicature Act which swept away the old courts and established the High Court of Justice and the Court of Appeal also created the 'Official Referee'. The Official Referee was thought of as an Arbitrator but one whose tasks were related to issues where 'prolonged examination of documents or accounts or any scientific or local investigations' were required which could not 'conveniently be made before a jury or conducted by the Court or its Officers'.

Official Referees were appointed in 1875, a move which was welcomed by the lawyers, and after an initial hiccup over their fees, by 1880 the four Official Referees had more work than they could get through, and so it has remained since. Perhaps the limited fee of £5 for their services (now increased to a uniform £15!) had something to do with it, even though the Official Referee could only try issues and could not try a whole case and give judgment.

In the Arbitration Act of 1889 this was altered, the Official Referee being so permitted and also to act as an Arbitrator in a private arbitration, as under Section 11 of the 1950 Arbitration Act he still can, whilst the court could also refer an issue or a whole case to a private Arbitrator. Thus the Official Referees became indistinguishable from ordinary judges, although the title 'judge' was not bestowed on them until 1972. Their importance is that they were created to develop the legal innovation of a trial of complicated factual matters by a single mind alone, and this we have seen is coupled to the role of an Arbitrator.

But throughout the Victorian period merchants continued to be dissatisfied with the courts' procedures and both barristers and solicitors advocated reforms.

A letter to *The Times* of 11 August 1892 by an anonymous judge, but alleged to have been Lord Bowen, urged reform. Merchants, he said, were 'turning away from the courts, deterred by delays, technicalities and appeals. For such reasons and for other reasons of their own the mercantile public is not fond of law, if law can be avoided. They prefer even the hazardous and mysterious chances of arbitration in which some arbitrator who knows as much of the law as he does of theology, by the application of a rough and ready moral consciousness, or upon the affable principle of dividing the victory equally between both sides, decides intricate questions of law and fact with equal ease.'

This led to the creation of the Commercial Court within the Queen's Bench Division which hears commercial cases. Its creation was at first blocked by the Lord Coleridge, Lord Chief Justice, but he died in 1894, and in 1895 the court was set up.

During the twentieth century trial by a civil jury has been waning and has now almost disappeared except for the special cases first singled out in 1883. Perhaps this is because these are matters where judges are thought to be less knowledgeable than a jury of twelve, or perhaps here the law is of less importance than the views of the jury on facts or their approach to customary conduct.

Today, with Parliamentary activity producing thousands of pages of statutory law every year against perhaps a hundred at the turn of the century, knowledge of the complexities of the law plays a far bigger part in the trial of many civil cases and is thought to be beyond the average jury selected at random from the electoral role.

Perhaps there is a similar situation in relation to the technical (as opposed to the legal) implications of construction and other similar contracts which merits greater emphasis on trial by technical experts in the subject areas of the dispute.

However, it can be seen that it is only in the twentieth century that the traditional mode of trial in England by a jury has faded into comparative insignificance. (see Fig. 3.1).

Writing in 1949, Sir Patrick Hastings said, 'An English Jury is seldom if ever wrong. In my opinion twelve ordinary English men and women sitting together form the best tribunal the world has ever known.' Of course, he could charm surprising verdicts out of juries. He was a great special jury advocate and could get them to eat out of his hand.

But no one could be confident today that a jury would understand a complicated construction case which could take many weeks to unravel and which might also depend upon a certain knowledge of the performance of eccentrically loaded beams with high tensile steel in high

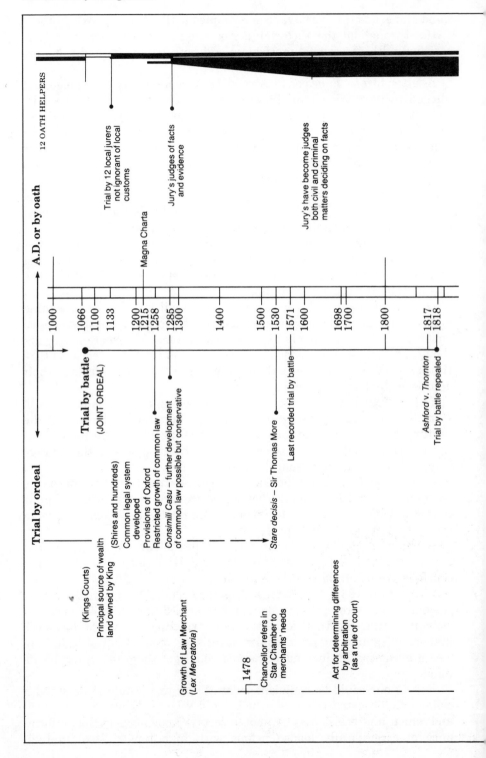

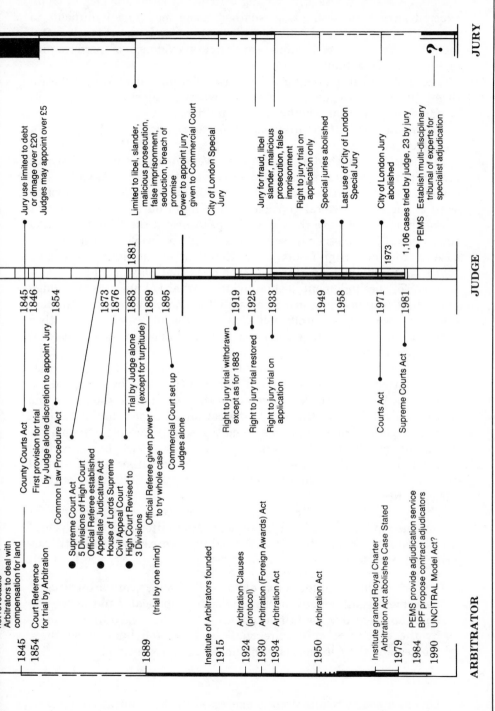

Fig. 3.1 Evolution of trial by jury, judge and arbitrator.

alumina cement. Worse still, having watched progress (or lack of it) on exposed sites in near freezing weather, some may find it difficult to accept that polythene sheets, hot air blowers and meticulously catalogued compression test cubes are weighty evidence of performance against a specification!

The problems in putting a wide range of technical matters before a (legal) judge may be just as frightening whether the sum involved is in hundreds of pounds or whether it is in millions.

So, should it be either litigation in the courts, or arbitration before a non-legal judge?

We have now reached a stage in the development of the courts where civil actions for small sums can be tried in the local magistrates or county courts, but if the amount at issue is in excess of £5,000 it must be tried in one of the several divisions of the High Court.

Solicitors do not have the right of appearance in the High Court and thus, even if for no other reason, counsel must be briefed to present the case in front of a High Court judge. Here there is no limit to the time that a case may take, and therefore the costs that may accrue.

Even so, once judgment is obtained from what is known as the 'judge of the first instance' it is not necessarily the end of the matter. English law being what it is, rarely will 'leave to appeal' be refused if either party, usually at this stage the loser, wishes to appeal to the next legal layer – the Court of Appeal.

Then, after further deliberations by each side's legal team, the matter, or matters, being appealed will be heard this time by three judges, all of them Lords of Appeal. Once again this may not be the end of the matter, for a two to one majority may permit an appeal to the Judicial Committee of the House of Lords – and there, until recently, the matter was at an end. But now that Britain is a member of the EEC, in certain circumstances further appeals can be made to either the Court of Human Rights in Strasburg or to the European Supreme Court in Luxemburg!

The benefits of an arbitration clause in a contract which provides for a final and binding Award, subject only to very limited appeal provisions, are clear to be seen. Section 16 of the Arbitration Act, which is still the principal Act, states:

> Unless a contrary intention is expressed therein, every arbitration agreement shall, where such a provision is applicable to the reference, be deemed to contain a provision that the award to be made by the arbitrator or umpire shall be final and binding on the parties and the persons claiming under them respectively.

and Section 17:

> Unless a contrary intention is expressed in the arbitration agreement, the arbitrator or umpire shall have power to correct in an

award any clerical mistake or error arising from any accidental slip or omission.

The basis on which an Arbitrator's Award can be set aside (or the Arbitrator removed) by the High Court is strictly limited by Section 23 of the Act to:

(1) Where an arbitrator or umpire has misconducted himself or the proceedings, the High Court may remove him.
(2) Where an arbitrator or umpire has misconducted himself or the proceedings, or an arbitration or award has been improperly procured, the High Court may set the award aside.
(3) Where an application is made to set aside an award, the High Court may order that any money made payable by the award shall be brought into court or otherwise secured pending the determination of the application.

The phrase 'misconduct' here means misconduct of the proceedings in the legal sense – not sleeping with the wife of one (or both) of the parties or their witnesses! It is a word continually criticised by judges and arbitrators alike, but it has remained even after the 1979 Act.

The 1950 Act also provided for any question of law arising in the course of the reference (the arbitration) or in the Award to be referred to the High Court in the form of a special case for the decision of the court – on a matter of law. The decision on the Award, which of course relates also (or more especially) to the facts of the case, remains the Arbitrator's province.

Because this proviso has been used in recent years purely as a delaying tactic to keep one party from his just rights – whilst inflation and high interest rates well beyond those subsequently ordered by the court made it worth the losing parties' while to do so, the 1979 Act has further limited reference from an Arbitrator's Award to the courts.

In the case of international contracts, i.e. those where at least one of the parties is foreign, the right to appeal to the English courts on a point of law can be excluded altogether, making the Arbitrator's Award final in all respects both as to law and fact.

Thus, it might be thought that 'the resolution' of construction contractual disputes under English arbitration had reached a stage of practical development where parties to a construction contract would be happy to submit their dispute and themselves to be examined in the privacy of the Arbitration Court by a technical Arbitrator, and then to accept his Award as final and binding. Thus expressing confidence that the arbitration procedure under English law fulfilled the six tenets set out by Italian Professor E. Minoli in 1972 as being objectively worthy of trust. These features he summarised as follows:

(a) the certainty of the application of arbitration on demand by one of the parties;

(b) basic equality in the positions of the parties before the arbiter;
(c) professional competence and impartiality of the arbiter;
(d) a reasonably fast and inexpensive procedure;
(e) the legal effectiveness of the arbitration award, even against the recalcitrant party;
(f) the reasonable certainty of the execution of the award.

Professor Minoli was concerned in particular with international arbitration and so with matters like the availability and enforceability of Awards by foreign governments. These were particularly significant considering the time and venue of his address (IV International Arbitration Congress, Moscow 1972). However, let us look now at the fundamental benefits of the arbitration process in the domestic situation.

All arbitration has two essential benefits to the parties. The first is privacy, and the second informality.

Both are conducive to a more relaxed atmosphere in which factual evidence, particularly of a technical nature, can be presented and evaluated.

Both help to reduce the stress of the action upon the individuals involved and reduce the stress on the parties' reputation in their general market-place compared with that to which witnesses are exposed by a trial in the glare of publicity and under the adversarial approach and attitudes of an open court with posturing advocates retaining their medieval role as the champion of their client's cause.

Twentieth-century application of arbitration in the UK

If we examine the areas where arbitration has been most used in the UK since 1900 we can identify three specific areas – Shipping, Construction, and the Commodity Markets.

Both Shipping and Construction have the common feature that they are concerned with a unique set of multi-contractual relationships. These produce one-off situations in which any financial differences must be resolved in relation to that specific contract, or charter-party.

In many commercial situations where buyer and seller trade together regularly over long periods problems that arise can more easily be sorted out as both parties have a vested interest in the continuity of the relationship. This is not so with one-off contracts.

Both Shipping and Construction are also particularly subject to unforeseen situations generally of a technical rather than a legal nature and are industries where custom and practice play an important role.

In Construction in the twentieth century technological advances also produce new problems in situations which in other industries would be regarded purely as prototype. Problems are expected to occur on prototypes and be dealt with within the framework of, and at the cost of, the one organisation producing the prototype. There the analysis of cause would be internal, thorough, private and objectively conducted – and cheaper.

In the case of construction contracts and shipping charter-parties the cost of these variations has to be met by one of the parties rather than collectively, but the benefits of a private tribunal to assess responsibilities and award costs is clearly preferable.

The third area in which arbitration has been developed has been over the quality of merchandise traded in the Commodity Markets. The markets for coffee, cocoa, sugar, jute, flax, cotton and wool have all had private arbitration schemes for many years. Indeed, by 1950 there were some forty organisations in the UK where rules of the market or trade association provided for disputes between merchants to be settled by arbitration. Many of these rules state that the Arbitrator should be 'a commercial man' or 'a technical man', or alternatively 'not a lawyer'.

The matter at issue in these situations concerns a bargain struck between two 'expert' merchants who are members of a small market where all merchants are known to each other and who deal with each other all the time. They will have struck a bargain over a particular consignment of, say, coffee, where the quality, price and perhaps delivery date will have been agreed upon whilst the crop is still growing, and certainly was not able to be readily inspected by the buyer. When the consignment arrives the buyer considers that it is not up to specification – the seller disagrees.

No amount of argument can produce a solution to what is essentially judging quality against some predefined or undefined standard. Therefore a third merchant equally expert and, indeed, one who may well have been involved in similar deals about similar crops at a similar time, is called in to decide between the merits of the parties' argument.

This decision must essentially be based on his view of the quality of the goods which is determined by his personal opinion based upon his own expertise, knowledge of the market, and of its particular customs.

These arbitrations, for obvious reasons, have become known as 'pinch and sniff'. Equally obviously, a lawyer, unless he was a trading member of the market, is not skilled at this kind of pinching and sniffing!

Once again, privacy is highly important both for the individual merchants and for the market as a whole. The parties do not want their disagreement over the quality as seen by expert merchants discussed in the lay press with banner headlines 'Merchant condemns coffee consignment', when the next day the merchant will be seeking to sell the coffee to an instant coffee manufacturer as top-grade coffee beans from the 1987 crop. Both situations could be predominantly true but valid contract communication depends here upon the understanding within rather than across cultures.

If such a dispute were referred to the courts experts for both sides

29

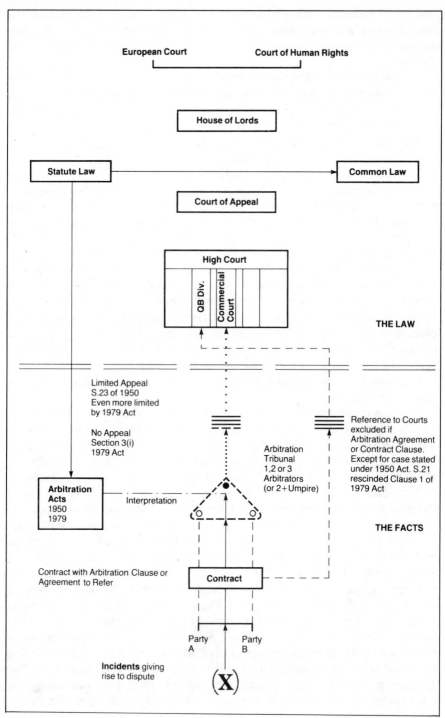

Fig. 3.2 The structure of English arbitration and its beneficial relationship to the courts.

would have to argue their case for quality in front of a judge who is required by his position to know nothing about the matter except that which is presented to him as evidence by lawyers, who would themselves have required a potted explanation of the habits of coffee growers in Brazil, the botanical origins of coffee beans, the customs of the market, the methods of shipment, the prices reigning at the time the deal was struck, etc.

Privacy, speed, informality and the expertise of the Arbitrator all contribute to the use of the arbitration process rather than the legal process and the costs as a consequence are infinitely lower. Coffee being a perishable commodity it is highly likely that by the time the case came on in court the beans which had been retained as samples of the consignment would probably by then have justified the original banner headline and the consignment would certainly have been condemned!

Similar conditions requiring speed, informality, privacy and technical knowledge of quality, are present in construction disputes and in new areas of technology such as the computer industry where many matters are equivalent to the 'pinch and sniff' determination by the appropriate 'pinch and sniff' experts in, say, microchip technology.

All of these advantages to the commercial man, combine with the basic benefit that derives from the finality of the Arbitration Award which avoids the long legal route to finality, which is illustrated by Fig. 3.2.

Why then are parties reluctant to take the first steps in formal arbitration?

Is there not great scope for improvement?

I submit there is, and after a step-by-step analysis of the detail procedures I will put forward practical procedures in tune with current needs.

Benefits of litigation	Benefits of arbitration

Open court
  For precedence and the public
  interest
Equal right of representation
Case Law relevance
Integrity of Judge and legal system
Certainty of enforcement
Right of appeal
  To the Court of Appeal
  To the House of Lords
	Chief features worthy of trust
	  Privacy
	  Certainty of application
	  Equality of parties
	  Competence of arbitrator
	  Fast and inexpensive
	  Legal effectiveness
	  Certainty of enforcement

Fig. 3.3 Benefits of litigation and arbitration (E. Minoli – 1972).

CHAPTER 4

MANAGEMENT, MANAGEMENT FUNCTIONS AND DISPUTE RESOLUTION

Definitions of management reflect the approach of the author and range from the human to the mechanistic.

Construction Industry management involves all the classic functions of planning, organising, motivating and controlling, and requires definitions of authority, responsibility and accountability for all those involved in the process.

In Construction this includes the client, whose objectives must first be defined and the extent and manner in which these functions are delegated through the brief, the design and implementation stages of a project by means of formal agreements which create contractual relationships.

Human motivation and its relationship to behaviour patterns in 'normal' agreed situations and then in conflict situations suggest that the appointment by the parties of a third party to 'manage' the dispute or potential dispute situation is a technique which is likely to be successful if it incorporates 'management thinking'.

So far we have looked at the evolution of the Construction Industry and the fundamental reasons why disputes occur within it. We have looked at the law and its evolution and the concepts of arbitration that have arisen and been given the backing and support of the law through statutory instruments – Acts of Parliament – going back in the UK nearly 200 years.

Let us now look at the evolution of management to identify the validity of these doctrines for the better resolution of construction disputes.

Management definitions

There are as many definitions of management as there are of pundits. The definitions perhaps reflect the definer's management style or attitude as much as his analysis of the subject. Definitions range from 'getting work done through people – a social process' to the far more authoritarian and mechanistic 'planning and regulating the operations of an enterprise in relation to its procedures and to the duties and tasks of its personnel'. The International Labour Organisation in 1937 defined management as:

1. The complex of coordinated activities by means of which an undertaking, public or private, is conducted.
2. Organisation: the complex of activities the object of which is to achieve optimum coordination of the functions of the undertaking.

The first, 'getting work done through people', was that given to me over lunch in the mid–1960s by Dr J. F. Dempsey who was then the Chairman of the Irish Management Institute but who was in 1936 one of the founders of the first Irish aeroplane company which he later developed as Aer Lingus and of which he was then its Chief Executive. This was a position he had held for most of the time since he was first involved with the company – when a single De Havilland Dragon aircraft was carrying six passengers on a daily trip of 200 miles between Dublin and Bristol.

Those who have observed the promotion of Aer Lingus will know that it described itself as 'The friendly airline', and those who have flown Aer Lingus will know that whatever other attributes it had, the airline staff, now 5,000 strong and flying many millions of miles every year on daily schedules to every continent and most developed countries of the world, certainly reflect that adage. James Dempsey's attitudes, personality and influence were clearly reflected in the management of Aer Lingus.

Now the law itself, and certainly the common law, reflecting the customs and practices and established ways of the community in which it was based, could be considered 'a social process'. But established ways reflect and encourage the conservatism of the British, and progress, or evolution, of the law in turn reflects the slow way in which social change develops.

If we look at another definition of management which seems to me to be appropriate to the Construction Industry, 'The direction of men and materials to a given end', we can recognise more easily the implications of technique or scientific method which springs from the origins of modern management through 'work study' as developed by Taylor, Gilbreth and others. They realised that the development of techniques to improve performance required first the development of appropriate measuring techniques. Techniques to measure input against output, and the balance of requirements against resources, so that productivity can be established and better ways found to improve performance within an organisation.

The finer measurement of performance in both physical and people systems was necessary and new terms and concepts needed to be identified to be able to communicate the results and develop an understanding of them to other people, and perhaps for the first time across disciplines.

Work study produced terms such as 'Therblig' (Gilbreth backwards), work measurement, standard performance from standard rating, relaxation allowances, predetermined motion time systems, activity sampling, critical path networking, etc. and these reflect that management systems are technical systems for the direction not only of men but also of materials towards the stated objective. In the Construction Industry the application of materials embraces also the operation of machines and methods, which latter all have financial implications.

The direction of men may be assisted by financial incentives, but in today's social structure motivation involves far more than just money. Today a literate and highly numerate community have greater freedom of choice, as a result of economic progress, as well as the Roosevelt/ Churchill wartime mid-Atlantic pronouncement on international and natural freedoms.

We have freedom of trade and of speech, freedom to worship, freedom of political association amongst the principles drawn up in 1941 by the Atlantic Charter. More recently under the 1984 Trade Union Act there is the freedom to belong or not to belong to a trade union.

Motivation means more than just money for workers in the latter part of the twentieth century.

Management in the construction process

In Construction there is an essential difference in the application of management principles, in that a construction project has a finite life. It has a beginning – with the establishment of the need – in detail – in the client's brief. It has a middle – the design and development of the solutions to those needs – and an end – the implementation by the contractor of the solution in terms of the physical construction of the building. After which, the project's people structure and the other physical resources which have been employed are broken down and redeployed on other projects under other managers for other organisations. But the fundamental principles still apply.

Figure 4.1 illustrates how managers must so organise their five management resources of men, materials, machines, methods and

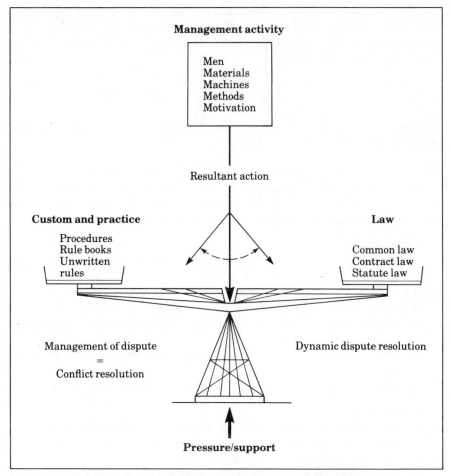

Fig. 4.1 Management balances between law and custom and practice
(First published in Asian Building and Construction June 1985).

money within the framework of the law on the one hand, and within the established customs and practices on the other, to achieve a balance and harmony through which the stated objective – generally the construction of the client's building – could be economically achieved.

Management must therefore produce a cohesive body of knowledge which is logically arguable, if not yet always scientifically provable.

Figure 4.1 also suggests how the manager in Construction must apply his effort to keep the balance whilst appreciating that if the result of his management action lies outside 'the middle third' of what is inherently an unstable body the structure will overturn!

Again, if the pressure applied is unevenly spread, or too pointed, the stress set up in the structural elements of the organisation could be so great as to cause a failure in the member by sheer (or is it shear?) stress.

It is interesting to reflect that we find ourselves using terms established in scientific areas such as physics for the description of human or social problems. It is not only in the field of computer technology that a cybernetic* study is useful!

Functions of management

Whilst definitions of management are wide with regard to both its technique and philosophical limits there will be more general agreement on the functions and principles which must be practised to achieve success. These functions can be analysed for the manager as follows:

1. **Planning**
   (a) Forecasting the future so that the enterprise may be in a position to continue to operate effectively.
   (b) Setting the objectives – for the workforce under his control.
   (c) Defining the policies whereby these objectives will be achieved.
   (d) Establishing the outline procedures through which these policies will be implemented.
   (e) Preparing the budgets for the financial implications of these policies.
   (f) Scheduling the tasks involved in carrying out these policies.

2. **Organising**
   (a) Developing a system within which individual efforts can be harnessed together in the most effective way to produce overall momentum to the organisation.
   (b) Delegating his responsibility for particular areas of the operation and giving with it the authority to control these.
   (c) Establishing relationships between those involved at different levels in the organisation structure on a formal basis.

3. **Leading and motivating**
   (a) Making decisions which affect himself and other people.
   (b) Selecting those with whom he will carry out his tasks.
   (c) Training people who will have to work within the organisation.
   (d) Understanding people, their own mainspring, their personal objectives, self-motivation and will to work.
   (e) Developing the environment which will stimulate individual action and responsibility.

* 'Cybernetics' from the Greek *kybernetes*, a steersman, or 'governor', a term invented by Norbert Weiner, Professor of Mathematics at MIT. A study of the way the human mind works related to the development of computing machines, the theory of messages, communications and control engineering. The relationship between machines and living organisms.

(f) Establishing effective communication within and outside his organisation to ensure that confusion does not arise.

4. **Controlling**
   (a) Setting standards of performance.
   (b) Measuring standards of performance.
   (c) Assessing the results of progress.
   (d) Taking corrective action where this is necessary as a result of deviation from the standards.

But how do all these apply to the Construction Industry? In the dispute situation? Who is the manager? Who the managed? What are the manager's resources? And what is the project objective? Will this not vary depending upon whether we are looking at the position from the point of view of 'the client' or building owner? The architect or engineer consultant or the contractor? And to what extent might these same functions relate to an Arbitrator?

Furthermore, what, if any, of this analysis applies to the contract, that is the set of legal promises which the parties have entered into to bring about the fulfilment of the client's building needs?

Figure 4.2 analyses these management functions in a series of checklists which I have used when examining disputes that have come before me as Arbitrator. They help to establish standards which could be expected to have been used in setting up the management structure and performing the tasks required for the completion of the project by the 'agreement' which has itself been evidenced by the contract documents – that is, **all** of the contract documents: drawings, specifications, schedules, networks, programmes, and not just the printed standard 'JCT' (Joint Contract Tribunal) or other forms, or their variations.

Those managing a building project must also recognise a number of other fundamental principles of management and see that they are implemented in turn by all those involved in the project.

In a building project, unlike many other management structures, the top management is frequently, one might say generally, amateur in that the task is performed only once, or at most very infrequently, by the client building owner. The remainder of the management team, as we saw in the introductory Fig. 1.1, are all professional, and expert.

Then there is the further division between 'professional consultants' and 'commercial' contracting activity, and the functions performed by these groups in separate corporate organisations but coming together in a variety of project arrangements to fulfil the client requirements for the project.

It is this nexus of human relationships that becomes a nexus of contractual relationships, that is at the root of many dispute situations. Far more disputes arise through failures in organisation and in the communications between the different groups than result from failures

Management function	Checklist for contractor's organisation	Checklist for 'one-off' contracts – client area	External and 'third party' factors
1. Planning			
Forecasting	Were reasonable or impractical forecasts made?	Were these factors entirely in the hands of the contractor or were they mandatory upon him by 'client'?	Was appropriate or necessary or economic or technical data available and considered?
Setting objectives	Were the objectives achievable in normal circumstances?		
Defining policies	Were the policies inevitable or was there a range of choice?	Were any of these matters for joint participation between 'client' and contractor?	Who formulated the terms? Was the contract competitively bid for? or negotiated?
Establishing procedures to implement the policy	Were these simple and capable of reasonable adaptation in the event of accident?		
Preparing budgets	Was the financial basis tight, and so were the budgets too stringent without margin for error?	Were Q.A. procedures required?	
Scheduling tasks	Were these thorough and comprehensive?	Was Client included?	And the Architect?
2. Organising			
Developing a system	Were the individual efforts harnessed to produce effective overall momentum to the project/or organisation?	Were any of these matters subsequent to the signing of the contract influenced by the 'client' or anyone in his organisation?	Changes in Government? Changes in Statutes?
Delegating responsibility	Was the authority appropriate to the responsibility given to the people involved in the specific operation or area of activity?		
Establishing relationship	Were the right relationships established between the people involved in the operations and at different levels within the organisation of the contractor and with those involved in the operation but outside the contractor's own staff or contract?	Could the client's organisation have disturbed these factors through actions or inactions of his own staff or directors after the contract was in progress?	Changes in company structure or legal relationships? Were outside authorities requirements or attitudes adequately considered?

3. Leading and motivating

Making decisions	Were these sound and firmly made?	Was the client involved, did he influence, or be influenced by these matters?	Was their influence changing? for better or worse?
Selecting people	Were the right kind of people selected for the different tasks?	Were his own people adequately aware or trained to play their part in the contract properly?	Were social conditions generally in step with those envisaged by the situation of the contract.
Training	Was adequate training given for new or developed tasks?		
Developing the work environment	Was adequate attention given to providing suitable working conditions or incentives to encourage effective performance by those involved?	Did the client or his servants improve or worsen these conditions?	1 If all matters in the three areas above had received proper attention in the planning and organising stage then were adequate standards for control set? Was planning done before contract was entered into, or afterwards?
Establishing effective communication channels	Did those involved in the operations have access to information on the involvement of others in the process the overall objectives of the organisation and the purpose of the project, were they able to 'feed back' their own contribution to improve the overall performance as well as their own?	Were there any obvious areas of conflicting objectives?	
Understanding people	Were the individual motivations and will to work understood or did the framework of organisation put unnecessary stress on an individual's 'main spring'?	What did client do to minimise effect of these conflicts? Were they known before contract was signed or were they hidden or disguised?	

4. Controlling – Upon a 'happening', unplanned for, unforeseen or unlikely that affected the operations – what did the parties do?

Set standards	Were performance standards (technical in specification and in human job mandates) adequately designed?	What did client do? What did he try to do? What could he have done? What did he succeed in doing?	What did the contractor do? What did he try to do? What could he have done? What did he succeed in doing?
Measure standards	Was monitoring both as to quality and quantity carried out?	What standard did client expect? Was it quantified?	What standard did contractor envisage. Was it quantified?
Assess results	Was an assessment made of deviation from planned progress or performance within permitted tolerances?		
Take corrective action	Was action taken to correct the position? If it was not, was it quick and firm enough?	Was action influenced by external factors?	Climatic, economic, political climate?

Fig. 4.2 (a) Analysis of Management Functions in relation to matters before an arbitrator (a paper presented in Moscow by R. Baden Hellard to the IVth International Arbitration Congress).

Function	Arbitrator/adjudication area	Parties area
Planning		
Forecasting	Limited. Ensure own and parties' availability	Comply with directions
Setting objectives	Earliest resolution within economic limits for **both** parties	To win at all cost? To settle? To co-operate? To speedily resolve?
Defining policies	Decide on style of approach appropriate to nature of dispute, context, amount at issue, etc.	To be represented? Supported?
Establishing procedures	Highly important practical steps that will ensure policies are implemented	Establish procedure to match Adjudicator's directions
Preparing budgets	Could be very practical if parties are prepared to accept limits and directions. Award (and interim awards) would then control	Cost awareness could help to resolve dispute
Scheduling time	Could be an important element of Adjudicator's directions	Sub-scheduling to comply (not accept lawyer's limitations)
Controlling		
Setting objectives	Implicit in establishing procedures – Truth ? !	
Measuring objectives Assessing results from progress	Seeing directions are complied with	Seeing that the dispute resolution procedures take precedence over other matters
Taking corrective action	Awarding costs during progress of dispute if one party deviates from directions, and ensuring they are paid at the time, if appropriate	

Why should failure to comply with Adjudicator's direction not be corrected (by costs award) at the time deviation occurs? This ensures that equality is maintained between the parties – (counsel seeks a 'refresher' from time to time!)

Leading and motivating		
Making decisions	The end product of the Adjudicator's function	This will depend upon whether there is an intention at the top to resolve quickly and cost effectively or whether someone in the organisation (who?) wants their 'pound of flesh' or emotional satisfaction!
Selecting those to assist	Assessors Experts who will assist	
Training	Guidance on the way to first time disputants	
Understanding people	Implicit and very important	
Establish effective communication	Very important throughout and particularly at Hearing – adequate formality to suit case	

Adjudicators 'style' should reflect the whole concept of leading and motivating to bring about early resolution. 'He's in charge' – and will manage the operation!

Organising		
Developing system	The context and Adjudicator's approach to the early RESOLUTION, which is the objective of adjudication.	A mandate to 'settle' or 'agree' is essential or highly desirable if 'tactics' are to be consistent and the best case is presented
Delegating responsibility	NO – unless technical judgment on some technical aspect is delegated to a technical adjudicator who is a member of the tribunal and not an assessor	
Establish relationships	Hearing procedures and Arbitrator's style does this	

If the Adjudicator has identified his management purpose strongly enough as the earliest, economic, but fair and just, resolution of the dispute, perhaps it is possible to get **both** parties motivated behind that objective as a management task to which they must both contribute within the framework set out by the Adjudicator – irrespective, or almost apart from the outcome of the Award. The costs will be less and maybe some other levels of agreement on the technical facts at issue will emerge, when the 'adversarial' context is reduced.

At worst strong, firm and fair leadership from the Adjudicator will not exacerbate the differences accentuated by a totally adversarial environment and procedures.

Fig. 4.2 (b) The functions of management in a dispute situation.

41

of technology, materials, or even from the situations which develop from unforeseen events.

Before any functions can be carried out each manager at every level in the management pyramid must have defined for him his authority, his responsibility and his accountability.

Initially, within the client organisation this concept must be used to establish and define the client's objectives for his building. These should be crystallised in 'the architect's brief'. It should recognise the relative needs or wishes of the client in terms of function, aesthetics, cost and time requirements.

The establishment of the brief requires skill and in this the client has not had the opportunity to develop the skills needed. The establishment

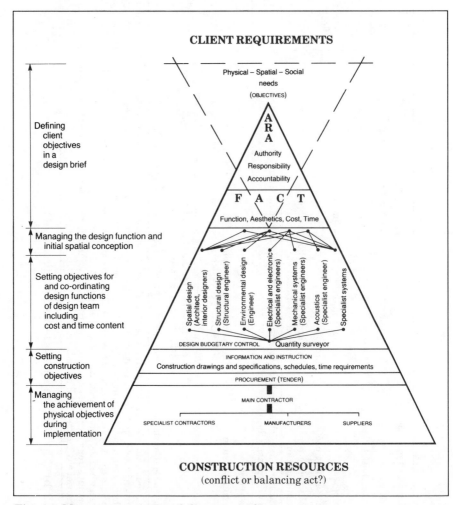

Fig. 4.3 Management responsibility pyramid –
building design and construction functions. Balancing requirements against resources

of the brief must therefore be an interactive process between the architect or engineer and the client. The brief should not be too determined, as this could frustrate the architect's ingenuity and his ability to create an original, imaginative and effective solution in four dimensions – time being added to the spatial concepts.

Figure 4.3 illustrates as a functional management responsibility pyramid the development of the project from initial concept into a detailed design for eventual implementation on site by the construction team.

Establishing the brief – whose responsibility?

The successful fulfilment of the client's needs requires progress through several distinct phases.

First 'getting the brief' is an interactive process between the client and the designer or design team. The client's physical, spatial and social requirements must be analysed into what might be considered in management terms as the 'design objectives'. These I have set down as the:

> Function
> Aesthetic
> Cost and objectives,
> Time

all of which should be expressed but given a priority or a 'weighting' so that at least one is 'open-ended'. At a later stage the client must consider all the functions.

- **Planning** – which involves forecasting his future needs.
- **Organising** – deciding who is to be involved and to what extent delegation of functional responsibilities is to be made. Is there to be a project manager? Or will the architect carry these responsibilities during the initial conceptual design stage? And through into the detail design stage? Or beyond?
- **Communicating and motivating** – is this function to be fulfilled by the client, or someone in his organisation, or is a specialist to be appointed, or will it be the architect or the contractor who is given the task, and who will then be responsible for controlling the operation?

Looked at in management terms, it becomes clear that there will also be contractual implications arising from the decisions taken, and indeed it is a lack of clarity and definition during the 'brief-getting' exercise which frequently is at the root of many disputes arising out of construction projects.

43

Controlling the design

The next stage illustrated by the pyramid is the need to coordinate and control these four facets of function, aesthetic, cost and time when the responsibility for the design development is delegated to the various specialist designers.

It is virtually impossible to delegate the overall initial conceptual design to other than one mind – the architect who creates at least in outline the client's total spatial objective – the whole building – after first having analysed all the client's functional requirements and also considered the constraints imposed by the site, the cost and the time limits.

In the process he will have created a three-dimensional solution which will have its own aesthetic, hopefully in balance with or fulfilling the client's objectives in this area also.

This outline design, or in management terms a 'feasibility study', should then be considered by the client in relation to all the objectives stated in the brief, at which point many previously unstated objectives or desirable criteria often emerge which should be at least given a hierarchy of desirability before the architect or overall designer restates them in the form of detail design objectives to the other members of the design team who will then be responsible for their detail development.

Controlling the cost

The management role of the quantity surveyor is frequently misunderstood, and at this stage his role is a 'staff' one rather like that of a budgetary controller, and at no stage during the design can it be an executive or 'line' relationship. That is to say, the quantity surveyor measures and assesses the likely cost implications of each part of the design and reports these back to the designer, particularly where they show a likely deviation from the initial cost plan or design budget. The specialist designer must then take whatever corrective action is open to him, or the overall design co-ordinator (the architect?) must amend the overall design or seek a fresh mandate from the client.

Having reached agreement on the function, aesthetic, cost and time balance at the completion of the detail design, the necessary information on which to obtain a tender can be prepared. This can then be put in front of a contractor or contractors in a suitable form so that they can bid, and in turn put their 'offer' before the client. Then, if any offer is acceptable in terms of time and cost, the tender can be accepted and an agreement then drawn up for the implementation of the client's defined objectives on site. This process of tendering should not, however, be the first time there has been a conscious recognition of the need to clarify the objectives as they have evolved in the design process.

Inherent in the taking of instructions – of any kind – are three processes: 'obtain', 'assess', 'accept', and these should have been applied at each stage of the sequential design process (see Table 4.1).

Table 4.1

RIBA plan of work	Progress stage	Task	Responsibility
Stage A	Primary brief	Obtain	Architect
A	Feasibility	Assess	Architect and building owner
A	Initial report	Accept	Building owner
B, D	Secondary brief	Obtain	Architect and design engineers
C, D	Outline proposals	Assess	Architect and design team
D, E, F	Scheme design	Accept	Building owner
E, F, G	Detailed design/ specification	Execute	Design team
H I	Tender documents	Assess Prepare bid	Contractor
	Bid or 'offer'	Assess/ Accept	Building owner
K	Construction on site	Implement	All contractors

Once again we see emerging the need for good management to balance (client) requirements against (construction) resources. This must be given full consideration and total objectives must be identified at this very early 'brief getting' stage when the fulcrum is high (in Fig. 4.3) and the balance can be seen to be precarious. This is a matter of some importance to both client and designer, and perhaps too the professional indemnity underwriters! (see Ch. 9).

In chapter 8. I will return to this theme of management balance for a deeper study of procedures to prevent disputes developing.

Management and the building agreement

When a building project is sent out to tender and a contract is entered into the basic assumption is that all of the many decisions have been made which are necessary to give effect to the building solution of the client's requirements. The contractor has been offered the opportunity to quote his price and time conditions for executing the work in a tender on which basis the contract is entered into. All will recognise, as do the normal forms of contract, that variations will occur.

The legal principle which is enshrined in the agreement is that it is a fair contract freely entered into between both parties – the building owner 'employer' and the contractor. The agreement therefore assumes at the time of signing that the objectives of the various parties involved are as one, or at least that a fair balance has been achieved.

The employer has defined, or has had defined for him by his design team, the size, shape, quality – or as Vitruvius had it, the 'commoditie firmness and delight' – that he requires, and by accepting the tender what he is prepared to pay for it.

The contractor, on the other hand, knows what is expected of him and when, and what profit he is aiming to make from the project for the effort and resources he has planned to commit to his tasks.

But new situations develop, both as unforeseen events happen and also because the client, building only once, can change his mind as he has second thoughts or sees new opportunities open before him.

The contract provides for amendments to be made and prescribes procedures for such variation orders to be issued so that they do not vitiate the contract. It has also been customary to provide that any differences that result between the employer and the contractor be resolved by the quasi-arbitration of the architect or engineer. But the law, as evidenced by recent judgments in the courts, regards the architect or engineer as the client's agent.

It is also frequently the case that the instruction needed and so provided through the medium of the variation order is necessary as a result of the fault or omission of the architect or engineer, or is the outcome of communication problems within the design team, which may in their turn be the result of communication difficulties between the client organisation and the design team.

The four directions for management application

In this situation of conflict we thus have an illustration of the difficulties in what is known as 'sideways management'.

There are four directions in which management flows. The most easily recognised is downwards from superior to subordinate – director to directed, boss to worker. The second is upwards, and every building professional knows that if he cannot 'manage' his client then he will not be able to control effectively the third direction for his management activity – inwards, himself and his own operating work functions. Every manager has two kinds of tasks – 'operating work' – that which only he can do, such as thinking, drawing, calculating, writing reports, etc. and 'managing work' – getting work done through others.

The fourth direction, that of sideways management, is readily recognised in large organisations as one fraught with difficulty. This is where colleagues of equal status and authority cannot agree on matters where their authority or influence overlap, or where their own planned objectives or procedures are in conflict with those of some other department. Normal management structures resolve this situation by reference upwards. Indeed, unless a manager has more than one subordinate of equal status beneath him his relationship to his subordinate is not that of a manager.

Management responsibilities **within** an organisation are generally defined in relation to structural diagrams showing also the authority and responsibilities of all those fulfilling management roles within the structure. Their contracts of employment or conditions of engagement provide, albeit implicitly, the contractual framework for the resolution of these problems which could otherwise become disputes. This is not to say they do not arise within large corporate structures, but they rarely become real problems for the supervisor/manager/ judge is aware of the situation, or he should be, and so able to take such action as his authority provides and the situation demands, and the sooner the better!

At the design stage of a building an overlap or conflict in responsibilities can frequently occur. The heating engineer wants to site a duct at a particular position in relation to the heating chamber, the structural engineer needs a column in the very same place, or perhaps for a beam to pass through the 'duct' space, whilst the architect, for visual and access reasons, wishes to have a glass door. All three designers have equal status – or at least their technical priorities seem to them of equal priority – particularly if all are working to a tight cost plan, and amendments to their design will cost more. Normally the architect as the co-ordinating designer adopts the role of supervisor/manager/judge and makes the decision between conflicting priorities. If, however, the client has separate contracts with each member of the design team a project manager would be needed to make the ruling.

The form of building agreement establishes an equality of relationship between the parties at the start of the project on the site.

But what when disputes develop?

In a building project we have seen that the organisation and relationship patterns stimulate the likelihood of dispute, when situations arise such as the discovery of poor footings where rock was expected, or when unexpected rock was found to be present where a void is to be created, not to mention the vagaries of the weather and actions of outside authorities!

A ruling is needed between the parties now in a 'sideways' management situation in which they could quickly become locked. The ruling of a project manager is hardly a valid concept. A relatively new function, the title and function may have been accorded to someone employed by the client to manage 'downwards' or by the contractor to manage 'downwards' and 'upwards'. But in neither case will he have the necessary authority to bind both.

In this situation, what is needed is someone whose authority is accepted by the parties, who can redefine or represent their 'objectives' to produce the balanced situation that was present in the first agreement. This would be essentially to achieve the completion of the client's building project as close to function, time and cost as originally stated, with satisfactory achievement also of the profit objectives for the contractor. Perhaps also to provide adequate sapiental satisfaction for the professionals from the performance of their design and supervisory tasks!

It is preferable that this authority should be exercised as soon as the difference has arisen. Successful football matches, from the point of view of player and spectator alike, result from immediate and firm decisions from the referee, whether these are to allow the game to continue and the players to find their own level or to penalise quickly or advantage one side or the other.

It follows that adjudication should be available immediately from someone outside the game and the players so far. He must be someone given authority by both sides and accountable only and equally to those separate parties. He will owe a duty of care to both, and not through an agency from one or the other with its consequent legal implications.

The BPF in 1983 analysed the management procedures of building projects as they saw them. They set up a multi-disciplinary working party with skills developed in all parts of the Industry which came to such a conclusion after many months of close study, it would seem, of both strategy and tactics.

They recommended, first, that better management and more thought at the outset of a project would reduce delays later. Next, that good communications and clear responsibilities within the design and development team could avoid future problems which cause unnecessary expense and delay; but nevertheless that it was also necessary to introduce the concept and role of an Adjudicator or, rather, two of them. The first, with duties related to differences between the design team and the second in relation to works on site.

I will return to this topic in depth in the later chapters in Part III.

For it is a concept whose time has come.

Management and motivation

Let us now look at the human element which is present in construction management situations; Dr Dempsey's 'getting work done through people'.

What motivates men? What motivates designers in drawing offices? What motivates men on a construction site? This will depend partly upon the conditions under which they work. There will certainly be different attitudes to working in exposed conditions in the summer with the temperature at 30 °C, to that in a similar situation in the winter at − 10 °C ... or will there? As far as the work is concerned there may be no difference! In both it could be to get the work done and get to hell out of it – or to reverse the order – until the temperature changes.

But the reaction of human beings, according to Maslow, depends fundamentally on the extent of their ascent up their basic pyramid (Fig. 4.4).

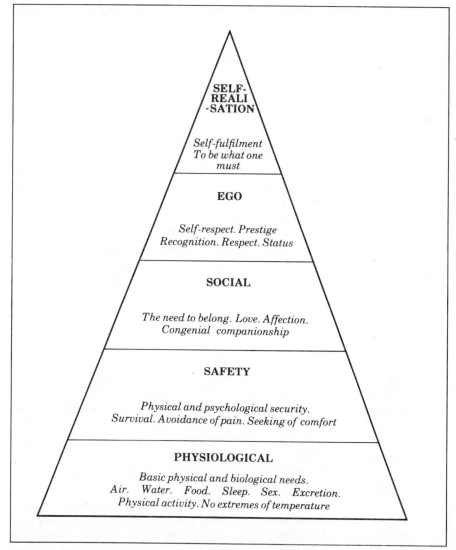

Fig. 4.4 Maslow's heirarchy of human needs.

Behaviour and motivation

Behaviour is the individual's total response to **all** motivating forces. One of which is the particular situation at a particular time, but Maslow suggests that all basic human **needs** can be expressed in a hierarchy of prepotency. That is to say, the appearance of one (superior) need usually rests upon the prior satisfaction of a lower or subordinate human need. The five levels in this hierarchy are, in ascending order: physiological, safety and comfort, social, egoistic, and self-realisation.

The theory postulates that man's animal wants are perpetual, and each drive is related to the state of satisfaction or dissatisfaction with the other drives.

Motivation is, however, human rather than animal-centred and is goal-orientated rather than 'drive'-orientated. All rational human behaviour is caused: we behave as we do because we are responding to forces that have the power to prompt – motivate – us to some manner or form of action. In a sense, therefore, behaviour *per se* can be considered to be an end result – a response to basic forces.

However, behaviour is actually only an intermediate step in a chain of events. Motivating forces lead to some manner or form of behaviour, and that behaviour must be directed towards some end. That is to say, there must be some reason why we are responding to the motivating force. And that reason could only be to satisfy the force which in the first place motivated us to behave. Consequently, all human beings, whether they do so rationally or irrationally, consciously or subconsciously, behave as they do to satisfy various motivating forces, says Maslow.

The forces that motivate people are legion and vary in degree, not only from individual to individual but also from time to time. They range from ethereal and psychological to concrete physical, instinctive, and basic physiological forces, such as hunger, thirst and avoidance of pain.

Motivation is not synonymous with behaviour. Motivations are only one class of determinants of behaviour. Whilst behaviour is almost always motivated, it is also almost always biologically, culturally and situationally determined as well. We are, in short, the product of our environment.

Undoubtedly, physiological needs are the most prepotent of all needs. In the human being who is missing everything in life in an extreme fashion it is most likely that the major motivation would be the physiological needs rather than any others.

If all needs are unsatisfied the organism is then dominated by the physiological needs; all other needs may become simply non-existent or be pushed into the background, for consciousness is almost completely pre-empted by hunger.

Attempts to measure all of man's goals and desires by his behaviour during extreme physiological deprivation are blind to many things. It is true that man lives by bread alone – when there is no bread. But, when there is plenty of bread at once other (and 'higher') needs emerge and these, rather than physiological hungers, dominate. When these in turn are satisfied, again new (and still 'higher') needs emerge and so on. That is what is meant by saying that the basic human needs are organised into a hierarchy of relative prepotency.

Thus, gratification becomes as important a concept as deprivation in motivation. It releases the organism from the domination of a relatively more physiological need, permitting the emergence of other more social goals.

When physiological needs are relatively well gratified there emerges a new set of needs, categorised roughly as the safety needs. As in the hungry man, the dominating goal is a strong determinant not only of his current world outlook but also of his philosophy of the future. Practically everything looks less important than safety. A man, in this state, providing it is extreme enough and chronic enough, may be characterised as living almost for safety alone.

Unlike infants, when adults feel their safety to be threatened we may not be able to see this on the surface. The need for safety is an active and dominant mobiliser of resources only in emergencies, e.g. war, crime waves, neurosis, and such chronically bad situations.

If both the physiological and the safety needs are fairly well gratified, there will emerge the love and affection and belongingness needs, and the whole cycle will repeat itself with this new centre.

All normal people in our society have a need or the desire for a stable, firmly based (usually) high evaluation of themselves, for self-respect, and for the esteem of others. Self-esteem is soundly based upon real capacity, achievement and respect from others. These needs are, first, the desire for strength, for achievement, for adequacy, for confidence in the face of the world, and for independence and freedom. Second, we have the desire for reputation or prestige (defining it as respect or esteem from other people), recognition or appreciation.

Even if all these needs are satisfied, we may still expect that a new discontent and restlessness will develop, unless the individual is also doing what he is fitted for. A musician must make music, an artist paint, a poet write, if he is to be ultimately happy. What a man **can** be, he **must** be. This need we call self-actualisation, the desire for self-fulfilment, to become everything that one is capable of becoming.

The specific form that these needs take will vary from person to person. In one individual it may take the form of the desire to be an ideal mother, in another it may be expressed athletically, in painting pictures or in inventions. It is not necessarily a creative urge although in people who have any capacities for creation it will take this form.

The clear emergence of these needs rests upon prior satisfaction of the physiological, safety, love and esteem needs. People who are satisfied in these needs are basically satisfied people, and it is from these that we may expect the fullest (and healthiest) creativeness.

McGregor's Theory 'X' and Theory 'Y'

Douglas McGregor takes this behaviour pattern on into what he postulates as Theory 'Y' – that people are self-motivated and will respond to what Drucker called 'management by objectives' in contrast to 'management by control' (Theory 'X') which he says results in people seeking to fulfil their social and self-fulfilment needs away from the job. Theory 'X', the more conventional management view, is that management is responsible for organising all its resources for economic interests and this means that people are 'directed' to fit the needs of the organisation. Without this firm direction people would be passive since they are by nature idle, lacking ambition and resistant to change.

Construction workers, perhaps because of their inherent job satisfaction – the carpenter who lavishes his skills on creating mouldings on doors, frames and staircases, the bricklayer whose prowess with an elaborate decorative brick bond – will be seen and admired by the generations that pass by his work, all appear to fit Theory 'Y' propositions better than they do Theory 'X'. Even more so many think that every architect and most designers are all the time engaged upon fulfilling their 'Y' needs at the top of the hierarchical pyramid!

But, because building construction, as illustrated in Figs 1.1 and 1.2, presents a basic situation where the progress of any project involves many people whose objectives are widely divergent or perhaps convergent and on a collision course, the behaviour of the parties is the result of these other factors present in conflict situations.

Cultural and group influences on Behaviour

But how an individual behaves will also depend upon his relationship with those other individuals with whom he is in daily contact.

In the nineteenth century the freedom of choice for the average worker was very limited. Economic freedom existed for very few beyond the employer. In the early days of the Industrial Revolution in the nineteenth century the individual could be considered to be hemmed in by the organisations and people around him (Fig. 4.5 (a)).

In the twentieth century economic conditions allow far greater freedom

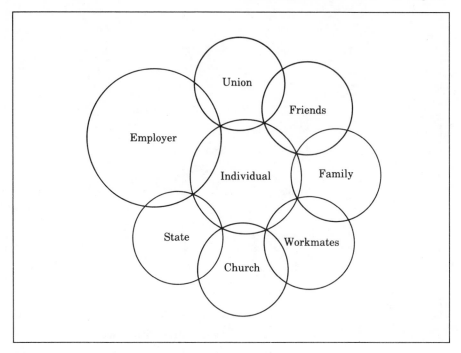

Fig. 4.5 The management of dispute.
(a) Influences on the employer/worker relationship in the 19th Century.

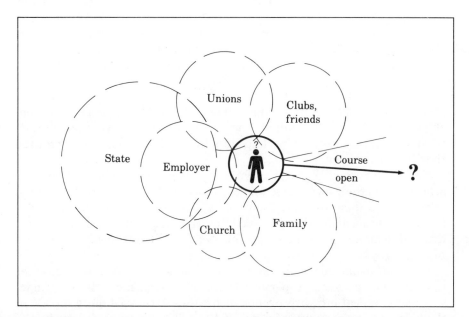

Fig. 4.5 (b) The individual is now less inhibited by 20th Century influences at the work place.

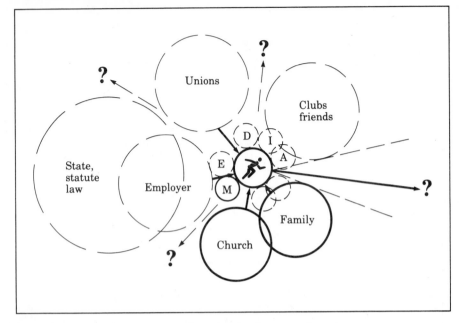

Fig. 4.5 (c)   Influences on attitudes to action in stress situations.

of action for the employed individual. The same circle of relationships between family, friends, church, trade unions, the employer and the State exist but their influence, either constraining or stimulating, has changed, at least as far as most individuals are concerned, from that experienced by a worker during the early Industrial Revolution (Fig. 4.5 (b)).

If we take this analysis one stage further into, say, a dispute situation in the 1980s, we find the position is different again. The relationships between the individual and the institutions, whether family, friends or authorities, are perhaps less immediate and influencing than they have ever been.

Since the Second World War children have been encouraged by their schools 'to do their own thing' and the economic climate of Britain in the 1980s allows them to exert their free will to choose, even if the choice has led to thousands of people spending thousands of pounds to become drug addicts, and so be no longer master of their own destiny and in a horrifying way!

But the media generally, and TV in particular, are now a greater influence on the average person. There is a much more direct, if one-way, communication, with events such as we witnessed daily on TV in the home during the miners' strike of 1985. The selection of shots by the TV producers to show horseback charges by the police against 'peaceful'

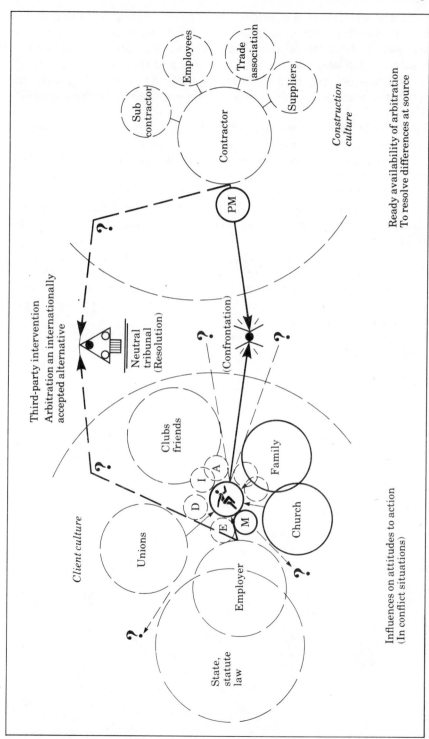

Fig. 4.5 (d) Influences and attitudes to action in situations of construction conflict.

pickets, and the throwing of bricks and flaming torches by these pickets, had more direct influence on a striking miner than the pamphlets or letters sent to him by his union leaders. Seeing is, after all, believing. The subtleties of selection, first by reporters and then by producers and by programme presenters, are not so apparent but clearly they have an effect on the viewing individual's attitudes and actions in these conflict situations.

Let us take this analysis one stage further and consider the likely implications on the two parties to a construction dispute. We can then see the benefits of the introduction of a neutral Adjudication Tribunal to bring about a solution to the dispute, providing that it recognises the management culture of construction and studies the contributory elements that caused the situation which may have flowed from materials, machines, methods or money, but takes account above all of the motivation of men.

Management philosophy tells us that what is needed is the giving of authority to the tribunal by the parties involved with some predefinition of their responsibilities but with clear accountability to *both* parties for discharging these responsibilities that had been given with *both* parties' authority (Fig. 4.5 (d)).

Chapter 8 shows how this management theory can be and has been applied in practice.

PART II

CURRENT ALTERNATIVES FOR RESOLUTION

CHAPTER 5

CURRENT ARBITRATION PROCEDURES IN THE UK

Arbitration, as the choice of the parties and the decision of the Arbitrator(s) selected will be upheld by the courts if conducted in accordance with the wide provisions of the 1950 and 1979 Arbitration Acts, the authority of which is related to the key elements of arbitration.

Quasi-arbitration under building contracts, the overall procedures under the Acts, and the role of the preliminary meeting, the Arbitrator's directions over the conduct of the reference, oral and documents only Hearings, the Award, its publication, are all discussed.

The giving of reasons, the likelihood of appeal against an Award, and the implications of an appeal are considered and related to the management style of the Arbitrator, the requirements for a practical solution to a business problem developed under informal conditions, with privacy, speed and economy but without disturbing the balance and so ousting completely the authority and jurisdiction of the courts, without which a UK Arbitrator's Award would not be enforceable.

Arbitration is recognised by the law in the UK both to give the parties freedom of opportunity to contract, that is to make agreements they intend to be legal, binding and within the law – and then to resolve problems arising from these agreements within a private and technical arena of their own choosing.

The principal Acts governing arbitration are the 1950 Arbitration Act, which was itself a consolidation of the Arbitration Acts of 1889 to 1934, and the Arbitration Act of 1979.

So the court will not upset an arbitration agreement entered into by the parties. Section 1 of the 1950 Act acknowledges the fact of arbitration agreements:

1. The authority of an arbitrator or umpire appointed by or by virtue of an arbitration agreement shall, unless a contrary intention is expressed in the agreement, be irrevocable except by leave of the High Court or a judge thereof.

Further, the court will stay any legal proceedings in the event that one party having already agreed to resolve any differences by arbitration seeks to change his mind and take the matter before the courts. Section 4(1) of the 1950 Act deals with this:

4(1) If any party to an arbitration agreement...commences any legal proceedings in any court against any other party to the agreement...in respect of any matter agreed to be referred, any party to those legal proceedings may...apply to that court to stay the proceedings, and that court...may make an order staying the proceedings.

Arbitration clauses

Parties may make their arbitration agreement at the time of signing the contract or principal agreement or enter into an arbitration agreement after the dispute has arisen. In the first case the contract should contain an arbitration clause such as:

Arbitration In the event of any dispute or difference arising between the parties out of or in relation to this Agreement the same shall be decided by an Arbitrator appointed by agreement between the parties or in the event of their failing to agree by an Arbitrator appointed by the President for the time being or the Vice President of the Chartered Institute of Arbitrators in accordance with the provisions of the Arbitration Act 1950 and 1979 or any statutory modification for the time being in force.

Similar clauses are frequently included in standard forms of contract of many kinds, particularly standard forms of building contract. Such special clauses nominate the president of some suitable institution or organisation as the person to appoint the Arbitrator in the event that the parties cannot agree upon the appointment of the Arbitrator. The current President of the Royal Institute of British Architects (RIBA), the Royal Institution of Chartered Surveyors (RICS), the Institution of Civil Engineers, the Institution of Structural Engineers, or more recently of the Chartered Institute of Arbitrators, are all examples of this reference to appoint by some neutral authority.

These special clauses are all aimed at giving effect to the basic intention behind an agreement to arbitrate, that is to make the agreement binding so that the benefits of a private and less formal trial before someone knowledgeable of the subject-matter of the dispute should be used rather than that the matter should go into court. In some cases the arbitration clause might go further and set out the rules under which the arbitration shall be conducted, thereby substituting those rules for the court procedures.

For example, the parties who wish to have a (domestic) dispute referred to an Arbitrator appointed by the President for the time being of the Chartered Institute of Arbitrators are recommended to insert in the contract an arbitration clause in the following form:

> Any dispute or difference of any kind whatsoever which arises or occurs between the parties in relation to any thing or matter arising under out of or in connexion with this agreement shall be referred to arbitration under the Arbitration Rules of the Chartered Institute of Arbitrators.

(Extract from Arbitration Rules of the
Chartered Institute of Arbitrators)

If the dispute is between two parties one of which is not an English company then the recommended clause should take the following form:

> Any dispute or difference between the parties in connection with this contract (agreement) shall be referred to and determined by arbitration under the International Arbitration Rules of the London Court of Arbitration.

(Extract from the Rules of the London
Court of International Arbitration)

Many difficulties, and much expense, can often be saved if the parties also expressly specify in their contract the law of the country by which it shall be governed.

If they choose English law, or if English law is for some other reason likely to apply, they may like to know that in most cases parties can, if they wish, exclude the jurisdiction of the English courts to review an Award or to determine preliminary points of law. An appropriate clause for achieving this result is:

> The parties agree to exclude any right of application or appeal to the English Courts in connexion with any question of law arising in the course of the arbitration or with respect to any award made.

This reflects the intentions of the 1979 Arbitration Act which has overcome many of the disadvantages which had developed under the 1950 Act, which I shall discuss later.

Format of Arbitration Tribunal

In UK construction cases it is normal to appoint only one Arbitrator to decide all matters. In construction cases overseas, particularly those through the International Chamber of Commerce (ICC), a tribunal of three is frequently appointed, whilst in the shipping area in the UK it is customary for each of the two parties to the charter-party or contract to name his own Arbitrator and then if a dispute occurs the two arbitrators meet together and in the event of their failure to agree on the Award over all matters in dispute to call in an Umpire to determine the award. In this case the arbitrators then become advocates.

For many years this position was thought strange and, indeed, wrong by construction arbitrators, but it should be realised that this procedure reflects the general conditions prevailing over a shipping dispute. Frequently, the contract would be entered into in London, perhaps on the Baltic Exchange, through agents for the parties who are at opposite ends of the world. The practical solution is to nominate an Arbitrator in London who can meet with the other Arbitrator in London, neither of whom had been involved in the particular contract or arrangements leading up to the contract. They will have agreed to their nomination at the time the contract was entered into but are independent and otherwise ignorant of its terms until having to consider a dispute that has arisen.

More often than not the two arbitrators are able to agree on the facts and upon their Award resulting therefrom. But if not, after having studied the matter, they are then in the best position to present to an Umpire both those matters on which they are already in agreement and then to advocate their own particular view on the matters on which they do not see eye to eye with the other Arbitrator and so seek the concurrence of the Umpire with their own view.

The Arbitrator/advocates present their own views on the situation, not the views of their appointing party. Indeed, sometimes it may not even be a view that is strictly in the interest of their appointing party. What they are in fact doing is getting a third individual's decision on those matters where, as arbitrators, they cannot agree on some particular item or items for the Award.

The procedure overall is a sensible and practical extension of the normal management functions of shipbrokers and others involved in the Shipping Industry and reflects a practical approach to resolving differences within an economic management framework.

Shipping arbitrations have nevertheless been carried out in the knowledge that if even this three-man tribunal procedure cannot produce an Award which both can accept the parties still had access to the Commercial Court – set up with this in mind in 1895. The arbitrators could be instructed to 'state-a-case' on matters of law related to the dispute (and the Award) and ask the court to rule. This has produced an interesting schism in that English arbitration over shipping matters was kept live and consistent by the reference to judgments under English law through the Commercial Court and thence, if necessary, reviewed, and confirmed or otherwise by the Court of Appeal and also ultimately, in those important but rare cases, by the House of Lords. This situation was held to be advantageous and one of the reasons why parties sought to have their disputes arbitrated in London under English law, but at the same time held to be disadvantageous in that the abuse of the 'case-stated' principle could lead, and has led, to delay and unwarranted expense.

Indeed, it was this feature which in an era of rapid inflation led to the abuse of the 'case-stated' principle and so to the pressure put on Parliament to enact the 1979 Arbitration Act. Its main purpose was to keep references to arbitration from overseas flowing into London – with beneficial economic consequences for the City of London, its lawyers, shipping and other experts, and arbitrators.

The architect or engineer and quasi-Arbitrator

In the Construction Industry it has been customary for standard forms of contract to nominate 'the architect' or 'the engineer' as a quasi-Arbitrator. It was thought that as the architect or engineer was not a party to the building contract he was therefore in this position of quasi-Arbitrator and able to determine matters in difference between the parties to the contract and that he would do so as an impartial and technical observer.

However, the architect or engineer is the agent of, or is in the employ of, one of the parties. Furthermore, the matter over which the difference or dispute arose could well be the result of the prior action of the architect or engineer. Whether this was a sin of omission or of commission or just an error or oversight would make no difference to the contractor, but at the same time the exercise of this power in such a position would require of the architect or engineer that he be 'judge-in-his-own-cause'.

Thus this situation, although in some ways an extension of the management practices in building contracts and somewhat similar to the appointment of two arbitrators in the shipping contract, is neither a practical solution nor one which when it has been tested has been found satisfactory to the judges in the courts.

If the provision for quasi-arbitration provided for in the form of contract did not work these contracts also provide for the appointment of an Arbitrator. This would not normally be until well after the practical completion of the project and the failure to agree a final account for it.

Then a suitable Arbitrator has to be agreed between the parties. Assuming one is selected and he is approached and is himself satisfied that he is competent to act and not prejudiced by reason of his past or present association or knowledge of either of the parties, he will accept formally the appointment in writing. He will, if he is sensible, also notify the parties of his fees and how he proposes that they be charged and paid. He will thereafter be in charge of all the proceedings.

Arbitration procedure

At this stage the Arbitrator may have only the barest outline of what the dispute is about, although there may well have been a written statement of the dispute from one of the parties, generally 'the claimant'.

Note that in arbitration it is customary to call the dispute 'the Reference', and the parties 'Claimant' and 'Respondent', as opposed to the terms 'plaintiff' and 'defendant' used in the courts. Sometimes it is difficult to decide which of the parties is the claimant and which is the respondent, and I have personally had one case where I helped the parties to decide which should be which! This was one of the matters which was settled at the Preliminary Meeting. It has some bearing on the matters at issue because it determines who should be first and who has the last word!

The Arbitrator will always first call a 'Preliminary Meeting' of the parties.

Preliminary meeting

The purposes of this meeting are:

1. Thoroughly to establish the terms of the submission to the Arbitrator. It is encumbent upon the Arbitrator that he must decide and make an Award on all matters that are in dispute – and these will be those expressed in the submission – but that he must not make any Award on any matter not submitted to him.
2. Issue by the Arbitrator of directions to the parties on how the reference should proceed from thereon.

The conduct of the preliminary meeting, like the conduct of all procedures in the arbitration, are matters on which the Arbitrator under the 1950 Act is given a great deal of power. Section 12 of the 1950 Act says:

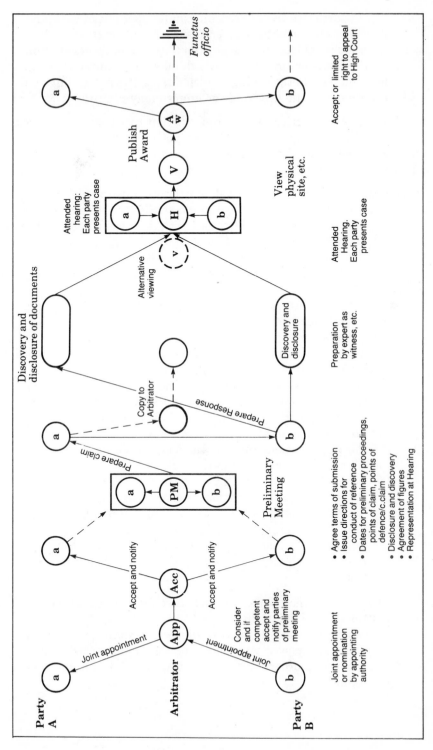

Fig. 5.1 The flow of arbitration procedures.

12(1) ...the parties to the reference...shall...submit to be examined by the arbitrator...on oath or affirmation...shall ...produce before the arbitrator...all documents within their possession or power...which may be required or called for, and do all other things which during the proceedings on the reference the arbitrator or umpire may require.

The Arbitrator has, particularly in construction cases, greater powers than a High Court judge. Where he does not have the powers of the High Court judge himself he has the facility to go to the court to obtain this power. For example:

12(4) ...a judge...may order that a writ of *subpoena ad testificandum* or of *subpoena duces tecum* shall issue to compel the attendance before an arbitrator...of a witness wherever he may be within the United Kingdom.

12(5) The High Court may also order that a writ of *habeas corpus ad testificandum*...to bring up a prisoner for examination before an arbitrator...

12(6) The High Court shall have...the same power of making orders in respect of:
(a) security for costs;
(b) discovery of documents and interrogatories;
(c) the giving of evidence by affidavit;
(d) examination on oath of any witness before an officer of the High Court or any other person,...the issue...or request for the examination of a witness out of the jurisdiction;
(e) the preservation, interim custody or sale of any goods which are the subject-matter of the reference;
(f) securing the amount in dispute in the reference;
(g) the detention, preservation or inspection of any property ...and authorising any persons to enter upon...any land or building in the possession of any party..., authorising...samples to be taken...observation to be made... expedient for...obtaining full information....

as it has for the purpose of and in relation to an action or matter in the High Court:
Provided that nothing in this subsection shall be taken to prejudice any power which may be vested in an arbitrator ...of making orders with respect to any of the matters aforesaid.

The Arbitrator's influence

The conduct of the proceedings will, however, reflect the personal style of the Arbitrator. Some arbitrators, having observed their conduct, tend to mirror that of a judge who sits for the most part silently watching and listening to presentations of counsel who, used to conducting matters in court, carry their adversarial approach and posture, shorn only of wig and gown, into the arbitration room. The Arbitrator thus sits po-faced and leaves it to each party's counsel to make the running. Thus the action proceeds until the Arbitrator eventually publishes his Award and no doubt then, if it is his wish, gives his response in his Award to the antics of the parties and their advocates during the progress of the reference. This could extend to allocating some particular part of the costs against any party who has been particularly dilatory or particularly extreme in taking up time unnecessarily.

Others take the view that the Arbitrator is there to manage the dispute to a just but early and economic conclusion. They therefore use their powers fairly as between the parties but effectively and sensibly in the light of:

(a) the matters at issue;
(b) the amount in dispute;
(c) the Arbitrator's own technical knowledge of the subject area – as it is this last point which has had an important bearing upon his appointment.

I take the view that the parties appointing the Arbitrator require him to be active and effective, and to use his knowledge and experience inquisitorially so as to see that the real issues and facts emerge as quickly and efficiently as possible. In short, to see that both parties get on with it and bring the matter to an early conclusion in the business interests of both of them. This assumes that the dispute is a matter which has arisen out of a business situation and is not one where one party's emotional or egoistic satisfaction is now the more important. Even then the Arbitrator's role is important in keeping matters in balance and seeing that the technical issues are properly dealt with.

The parties, after all, entered into their business agreement to bring about the achievement of business objectives. Initially they were as one on these objectives and initially they both set out to see that their particular part of the operation was managed to a successful conclusion.

One of the reasons for seeking arbitration in private rather than an adversarial battle in the public courts is to contain and resolve the dispute as closely as possible within the framework of the original business deal. The Arbitrator should therefore seek to manage and maintain, perhaps even restore, the balance that existed at the time of the parties making the agreement. As a first rule for his conduct of the

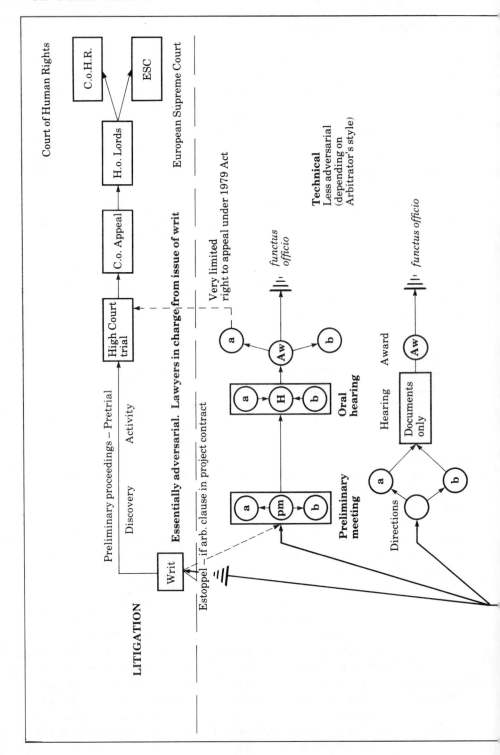

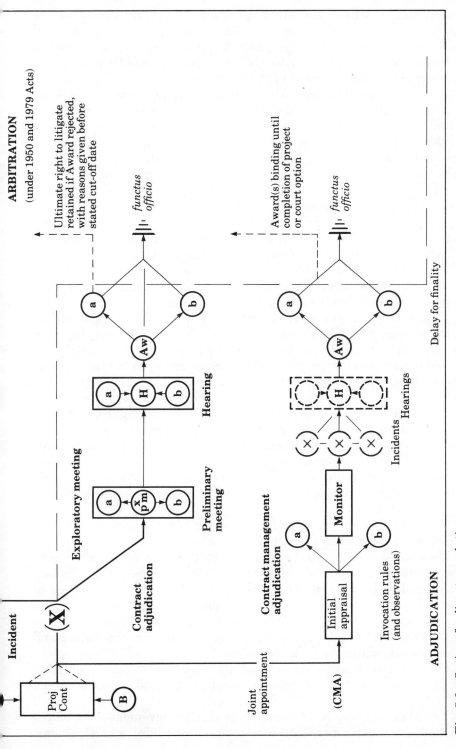

Fig. 5.2 Options for dispute resolution.

proceedings, I believe the Arbitrator must do nothing which will or might undermine the finality of his Award. Thus he will not do anything that will give the opportunity to either party to seek further reference to the court to set aside the Arbitrator's Award for any reason, and certainly not his conduct of the reference.

The Arbitrator therefore will not risk taking any action that could lead to allegations of misconduct, bias or unfairness to one party or the other.

With this in mind, the Arbitrator will then, at the preliminary meeting, draw up the programme for progressing the dispute. He may hear the views of both parties on each point of progress and procedure and even seek to get their agreement to his intended procedure prior to issuing his formal directions.

The possibilities of conciliation at this first meeting are great. Indeed, many disputes can be resolved at the preliminary meeting and the matter then settled by the Arbitrator issuing an **Award by Consent** that has been arrived at either between the parties themselves or by his using an approach akin to mediation, that is to say offering the parties help in arriving at their own conclusions and agreement.

He can help them to reach agreement but it is important that if this is the outcome of the preliminary meeting it should be properly finalised by the Arbitrator issuing an Award. In this he will see that it deals with all the matters that were in the submission or reference to him. Such an Award is the best possible outcome of any reference. Not only will it have been arrived at quickly, and by definition have returned the warring parties to a state of agreement, but it cannot later be upset or challenged by later action in the courts or elsewhere.

However, not all disputes will lend themselves to such expeditious treatment and the Arbitrator will have to go on to fix dates for the issue of the (detailed) points of claim by the claimant to the respondent. He will generally ask for copies of the points of claim to be sent to him at the same time.

The next date he will fix is for the points of reply and any counter-claims by the respondent.

If circumstances justify, he may also fix dates for points of reply to the counter-claim and requests for any further and better particulars, which will probably reflect the procedures of the court. But, bearing in mind it is the Arbitrator who is in charge of the conduct of the proceedings he may, if he feels it sensible and fair to do so, amend the procedures to fit all the circumstances of the case and the nature and extent of the matters to be investigated.

He will give instructions for the all-important 'discovery of documents' and ultimately he will fix the date for, and location of, the Hearing.

The Hearing may be held anywhere that is convenient – the offices of one or other of the parties, the Arbitrator's own office, a hotel, or even a cricket pavilion has been used. But this did not prove a great success for a particular Hearing in freezing midwinter, although it may well have done something to shorten the length of the proceedings!

The Arbitrator has great flexibility to issue directions on all these matters. This flexibility may be prescribed or limited by rules under which he has been instructed to conduct the case, for example, those of the London Court of Arbitration or the Chartered Institute of Arbitrators, but he will always have regard to fairness between the parties. For example, he will ask if one side intends to be represented by a solicitor or by counsel and he will make sure that the other side is aware of this and has the opportunity to be similarly represented if he should so wish.

Alternatively, it might be that the Arbitrator rules that neither side shall be legally represented. Then, if later one side wishes to be represented the Arbitrator may suspend the proceedings or delay them to enable the other side, should he so wish, to be similarly represented.

Just how far the Arbitrator can and should go in managing the proceedings I will consider again in Chapter 8.

In order to see that directions are complied with and that matters do progress as quickly as possible to a Hearing and then conclusion by the Award, it is my practice to make contact with the parties a day or so before a particular date has been fixed to remind them that I am expecting to receive a copy of the points of claim or defence or to receive a copy of the documents, etc. in order to let them know that the directions are to be complied with. If they are not – the cost of the delay will in any event be remembered in my Award when it will probably be held against the erring party. But, as I have said, not all arbitrators take the same view that their job is to manage the dispute to a speedy as well as just conclusion.

The Hearing

At the Hearing it is normal for the claimant to present his case first and to call his witnesses for examination in chief. After examination of each witness by the claimant or his representative, the respondent or his lawyer if he is so represented, will cross-examine the claimant's witnesses and then the claimant may re-examine the witnesses if he wishes only on any new point which has emerged in the cross-examination.

After the claimant has presented his case the respondent then has the opportunity to present his case, call his witnesses and have them cross-examined. Then the claimant has the opportunity of a final address to the Arbitrator.

The Arbitrator will normally allow the parties to conduct each stage of their own case, examine each witness and wait until the end of the cross-examination before himself raising points on which he feels he needs further information than that which has been given and on which he feels the particular witness could assist him.

The Arbitrator should not conduct the case for either side and should not therefore interfere with the way in which either party presents his case. However, the 1950 Act contends the parties shall submit to be examined **by** the Arbitrator and therefore if the Arbitrator wants to know something which the parties have not told him he is empowered to conduct that particular part of the examination himself and continue until he is satisfied – or not.

Evidence

The Arbitrator may have decided that the evidence should be given on oath, or affirmation, but he does not have to comply with the rules of evidence by which the courts are bound, although even they now depart sometimes from the strict rules, for example, in relation to hearsay evidence. The Arbitrator will, however, decide on the 'weighting' that he will give to any particular evidence and if he is an expert he is permitted to use his own knowledge of the subject-matter and of any evidence related to it.

In so doing he must be careful not to 'take his own evidence', that is to say use this special knowledge to introduce some matter into his thinking and reflect this in his Award if nothing has been said or produced at the Hearing. What he should do in these circumstances is to tell the parties what he has in mind and give them a chance to comment on it. His Award is not then likely to be upset, as was the Arbitrator's Award in the recent case where one side appeared before the Arbitrator claiming many thousands of pounds against a builder over a National House Building Council (NHBC) contract. The builder was in liquidation and so did not appear, nor did the NHBC. The Arbitrator's Award was for a few thousand pounds only – far short of the claim.

The claimant appealed against the Arbitrator's conduct of the case, saying that since no evidence was presented to the contrary the Arbitrator should have awarded what was claimed. The Arbitrator who, as it happened, was a barrister, a Fellow of the Chartered Institute of Arbitrators, a qualified surveyor and a Licentiate of the RIBA, said that he had used his own knowledge of what the cost of the work in question was, or should have been, and made his Award accordingly. The court, however, upset the Award saying that the Arbitrator, whether he was or was not an expert – and in this case they considered he had been appointed not as an architect or surveyor but for his legal knowledge – he had no right to 'take his own evidence' and use that knowledge without giving the claimant the opportunity to challenge or comment on that evidence if it was to be material to his Award.

It may be that the Arbitrator feels the case is being presented so far or obliquely from the matters that he sees to be at issue that in the interests of speed and economy or fairness to the parties he will conduct **his** examination earlier rather than later, but again bearing in mind that he should not do anything that could lead to anyone objecting to his Award on the grounds of his misconduct of the proceedings.

In practice this is probably easier to do than to write about. It reflects firm leadership from the Arbitrator rather than soft leadership and, as Maslow and McGregor tell us, there are times when either style may be more effective in particular situations and with particular people.

The Arbitrator's job, the responsibility he has under the authority he has been given by the parties, is to bring about a speedy, economic and just resolution of the dispute. He should 'control' proceedings and perhaps even 'lead' and 'motivate' the parties involved, recognising their individual human motivations. The way he conducts the whole proceedings might reflect the need for a 'leader' to develop the environment and provide effective communication channels in the confused state under which most construction disputes arise, and so restore the possibility for proper action. In my submission, in settling a construction dispute, management procedures are the more relevant for the Arbitrator and the parties than the legal precedent or procedures of the courts!

Written Hearings

Extensions of the use of arbitration have taken place in the 1970s into the field of consumer disputes and the arbitration of small claims; for example, arbitrations over disputes in the Travel Industry under the aegis of the Association of British Travel Agents (ABTA) and the Chartered Institute of Arbitrators.

I was fortunate enough to play some part in developing the organisation and establishing the procedures by which these disputes could be resolved. It was clearly impractical to bring witnesses from overseas holiday locations to give evidence about the state of the hotel room, the standard of food in the hotel restaurant, how bad weather restricted the availability of boat trips which were stated to have been features of a particular package holiday. The total cost might have been only a few hundred pounds, including an air fare, which itself might be more than half the cost. Yet, if the holidaymaker was aggrieved and felt he had suffered and lost much of the value of his only holiday of the year something had to be done.

This extension of arbitration into such small claims led to the practice of having an arbitration 'Hearing' based upon documentary evidence alone. In these cases the parties agree at the commencement that the Arbitrator is appointed on the basis that he will try the case on documents alone, in which case there may or may not be a preliminary meeting. But, the same principles apply; the Arbitrator will issue directions on how matters will be conducted, on what documents should be presented, on how each party will inform the other. In the case of documentary procedures, the Arbitrator's directions are even more important if the reference is to proceed to an early and effective conclusion.

I know of one case (not an ABTA one) where a documentary Hearing was agreed but where there had been fourteen exchanges of 'documentary evidence' over a period of 5 or 6 years which only stopped because the appointed Arbitrator died. Another Arbitrator had to be appointed. He decided after a preliminary meeting, attended by the parties to the dispute, that the Hearing should be a normal attended 'oral' Hearing. The matter then proceeded on this basis and was then resolved in about 3 months! Sometimes this can be the best – and the cheapest – in the long run.

There is, therefore, no reason why an Arbitrator should not, if he feels the circumstances merit it, have part of the Hearing based upon his scrutiny of documents beforehand and then the oral Hearing limited to a particular duration and directed to only particular aspects of the matters at issue.

The more technical the issues the more likely is this approach to be successful. Again, the Hearing might take place before or after a visit to the site which is the subject of the dispute, as it may be cheaper and better to take physical evidence than to have it presented by witnesses, expert or otherwise.

All these procedures are within the power of the Arbitrator, particularly the technical Arbitrator. It is, however, clear that often matters of technical fact and law are closely entwined or interdependent. For example, in relation to issues that have a statutory implication such as over Building Regulations, planning law and so on, and in a one-man Arbitration Tribunal, or perhaps even a three-man Tribunal, the Arbitrator may not feel he has all the knowledge necessary to draw up and finalise his Award.

If the Arbitrator is technical, then he is permitted to have the assistance of a legal assessor on points of law. Equally, if the Arbitrator is a legal Arbitrator he is permitted to have a technical assessor to assist him. In neither case, however, must the Arbitrator leave the decision or making of the Award to the assessor. It must be **his** Award.

The assessor may sit in on all or those parts of the Hearing for which his assessment is required, or the Arbitrator may put the points on which he requires the assessment outside of the Hearing, in which case he would be wise to inform the parties accordingly – again underlining that the Award is **his**, not the assessor's.

The Award

Having held the Hearing, the Arbitrator will prepare his Award in which he will set out his findings on all matters referred to him.

Under the 1979 Act he may be required to set out his reasons for his Award, whereas under the 1950 Act this was not normally the case. Arbitrators were advised 'never to give reasons'. This was because their reasons could then be appealed to the court. The purpose of the 1979 Act was to limit the reference from an arbitration or an Arbitrator's Award to the courts except in particular circumstances. The requirement to give reasons in such special circumstances was then written into the Act.

The Act does not, however, make the giving of reasons obligatory, and the late Lord Diplock, speaking during the debate on the third reading of the Bill (and when he was President of the Chartered Institute of Arbitrators) said:

> ...the Bill does not make the giving of reasons compulsory in all cases. In the great majority of domestic arbitrations in the commodity markets there is no dispute as to the law applicable; the question is a question of fact. They are what I described...as quality arbitrations.... (Hansard)

But the Act does give the court power to order an Arbitrator to give his reasons where an appeal is pending, but if the giving of reasons were to be mandatory in all cases there would have been no need to include such an express power. The Arbitrator is protected by the provision that in most cases notice that reasons will be required must be given *before* the Award is made. It follows that only in the most exceptional cases will reasons be ordered after an Award has been made.

The provisions for a limited – or controlled – right of appeal from an Award do presuppose that the Arbitrator's reasons will be available. As to how such reasons should be set out and what areas they ought to cover, to quote again from Lord Diplock's third reading speech:

> Another piece of reassurance which I can give is that when reasons are given they can be very simply expressed in ordinary language and not in the rather technical form which case-stated cases now take.

There remains the permanent problem with English arbitration to keep the balance between the parties to a commercial dispute who must not seek to oust the jurisdiction of the court but at the same time preserve the principle that an Arbitration Award should be final. If this were to be lost the main point and purpose of commercial arbitration would become so diluted as to be of little value to businessmen, and certainly overseas parties would seek to have their disputes settled outside England and English law. The 'special category' of cases therefore remains in the 1979 Act.

Publication of the Award

Having prepared his Award the Arbitrator will then notify the parties of its publication. Just how he does this will depend upon how the Arbitrator's agreement as to his fees has been prepared. He may notify both parties and tell them that the Award is available to be taken up upon payment of his fees. Either party (generally the one who thinks he has 'won') may then pay the fee and collect the Award, when the Arbitrator will then send a copy to the other party.

On the other hand, the Arbitrator may have made definite arrangements for the payment of his fees and so publish his Award by sending it at the same time to both parties or their solicitors.

Sometimes errors of arithmetic creep into an Arbitrator's Awards. Section 17 of the 1950 Act gives the Arbitrator powers to correct any calculation mistake or error arising from any accidental slip or omission, but that apart, once the Award has been published by the Arbitrator it is, in accordance with Section 16 of the Act 'final and binding on the parties and the persons claiming under them respectively'.

Functus officio

The Arbitrator is then '*functus officio*', that is to say he has completed his task. He no longer has any authority over the parties or the matters that were referred to him.

Enforceability of Awards

The 1950 and 1979 Acts deal with the enforceability of Arbitration Awards, both domestic (1950) and international (1979) in the UK,

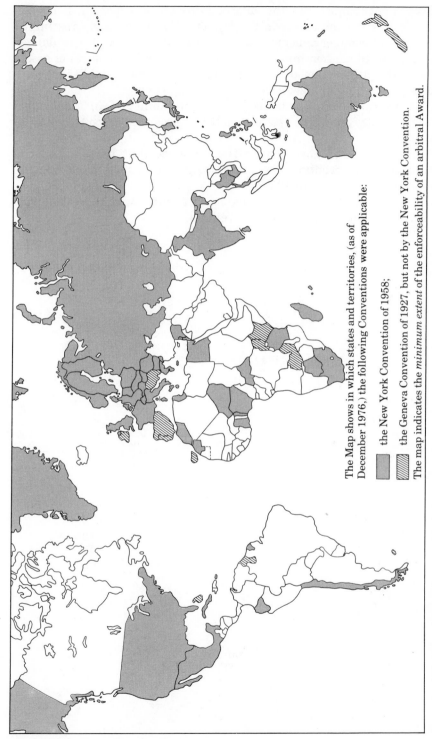

The Map shows in which states and territories, (as of December 1976,) the following Conventions were applicable:

the New York Convention of 1958;

the Geneva Convention of 1927, but not by the New York Convention.

The map indicates the *minimum extent* of the enforceability of an arbitral Award.

Fig. 5.3 World enforceability of arbitration awards.

Enforcement is much like the enforceability of court awards. It is even possible to have the assets in the UK of an overseas party restrained prior to the commencement of the proceedings if there is any danger that an Award against him could be frustrated by his removal of assets outside the jurisdiction of the UK courts. This was established quite recently by what is known as a 'Mareva' Injunction.

But with international projects the enforceability of an Award in a foreign country should be established before progressing too far with the proceedings.

Enforceability is governed by the countries that have signed the International Conventions for enforcement, the last of which was the New York Convention in 1958.

Figure 5.3 shows these on a global basis, together with those countries which signed the 1927 Geneva Convention.

CHAPTER 6

APPOINTING AN ARBITRATOR

The qualifications of an Arbitrator are immaterial to the courts (but not the parties) in supporting an Award, whether the Arbitrator is named when the main contract is signed or whether he or the Arbitration Tribunal is only appointed after a dispute has arisen.

The various methods and approaches to an appointment for both domestic and international construction disputes are considered and forms of appointment of some appointing bodies are illustrated.

The Arbitration Acts do not lay down anything about the qualification, selection or appointment of arbitrators. If the parties appoint someone who is not competent to carry out the task, but who does not commit any legal misconduct, although his Award may have neither sense nor reason, the courts will still not upset the Award. They take the view that the parties have made their decision, chosen their bed and so they must lie on it.

The arbitration clause in most standard forms of contract provides for the appointment of an Arbitrator 'by agreement between the parties, or in the event of their failing to agree, by a person appointed by the President or Vice-President for the time being' of whatever organisation or institute seems most appropriate to the sponsors of the form of contract.

Thus, the Presidents of the RIBA, the RICS, the Institution of Civil Engineers and the Institute of Structural Engineers are all named as the appointing authority in forms of contract in the Construction Industry.

In more recent years the President or Vice-President of the Chartered Institute of Arbitrators has been increasingly nominated as the appointing authority. This recognises that amongst the institute's 6,000 or so members, some 400 are arbitrators who have been trained by the institute and placed upon their panels but all of whom were, first, senior members of their respective professions.

Some of the other institutes maintain lists. In the case of the RIBA, its panels comprise only arbitrators who are also listed on the Chartered Institute of Arbitrators' panels – Grade I.

In some other cases a presidential appointment is made on a haphazard basis. The Arbitrator appointed may well be a very senior and experienced member of his profession but not one who necessarily knows much about the law and the procedures and practices of arbitration.

The Chartered Institute of Arbitrators does not publish a list of the members on its panels of arbitrators. Many of them are UK based and quite a large proportion are drawn from the Construction Industry. Some of these panel members are based overseas or will deal with overseas references.

The Chartered Institute of Arbitrators' panels were originally set up in the early 1970s under some thirty-seven headings, each of which was then subdivided into a 'technical' and a legal classification. In the Construction field these cover seventeen headings as follows:

Land/property
(a) Valuations; (b) structural surveyors.

Construction
(a) House building; (b) other building; (c) civil engineering;
(d) structural engineering; (e) specialist works; (f) mining;
(g) demolitions.

Engineering
(a) Mechanical; (b) electrical; (c) environmental.

Professional practice
(a) Partnerships; (b) professional/client; (c) inter-professional.

The members of the panels are further graded into two levels. They enter the first level after having passed the institute's examinations and then undergone a period of pupilage under an Arbitrator pupil master. After experience as arbitrators at the first level they may then proceed to the senior grade.

The Chartered Institute of Arbitrators maintain records of the appointments it makes. These now run into many hundreds a year and the institute also reviews from time to time the professional competence of these panel members.

No other organisation in the world has tackled this task of training arbitrators, except in Australia and New Zealand where branches of the Chartered Institute of Arbitrators have more recently followed along similar lines to those of the UK.

Thus Chartered Institute panel members will have undertaken a training course and have had to pass a two-stage examination and then gain experience with an experienced Arbitrator as a pupil master after many years of professional practice in their own calling, to establish their place on one or more of the panels according to their particular skills and experience.

But very few arbitrators spend all their time dealing with disputes. They, and the Chartered Institute, feel that it is essential that arbitrators maintain first-hand contact with their own profession, preferably by practising it, so that their experience is current in both their technical skills and in their arbitration procedures.

Where the parties have no knowledge of, or cannot agree on, a suitable Arbitrator, they can be assured that an approach to the Chartered Institute of Arbitrators will result in the appointment of a highly competent and suitable Arbitrator.

Appointing an Arbitrator in relation to overseas contracts

If the dispute involves a project and/or a client overseas similar provisions can apply, but as with all arbitration it is best to ensure that the potentiality for such an appointment is provided for in the main contract.

In these circumstances it is also important to make sure that the law of the contract, and the law relating to the arbitration agreement, does permit the procedure.

Very broadly speaking even a contract between an overseas State or State Agency can be referred to arbitration and the Arbitrator's Award will be enforceable if the State concerned has signed the Conventions of 1899 or 1907 or the New York Convention of 1958 which has some sixty signatories which accept the services of the Bureau of the Permanent Court of Arbitration in The Hague. But in practice the model rules produced by the Permanent Court are at the disposal of States who are members of the United Nations. This court has drafted a submission clause in the following terms:

> The parties agree to submit any dispute derived from the present contract or from those resulting therefrom to a procedure of
>
> a. arbitration
> b. conciliation
> c. conciliation, followed, in case of
>   non-conciliation by arbitration.

For this purpose the parties shall apply to the services of the Bureau of the Permanent Court of Arbitration at The Hague. They shall accept the 'Set of Rules on arbitration and conciliation in international disputes between two parties of which only one is a

State', elaborated by the Bureau in the year 1962; however, they will be free to replace the rules of procedure by other ones on which they should have agreed (alternatively: by the dispositions contained in the Annex to this contract).

The tribunal appointed by the bureau will normally be of three members selected by agreement between the parties or in the event of their failure to agree by the Secretary-General, who will also appoint them if requested by the parties to do so. These arbitrations, which will be over major matters, probably between a large international corporation and a State, will be held in the Peace Palace at The Hague. For lesser disputes and those where both parties are commercial undertakings, the ICC with its headquarters in Paris or the London Court of International Arbitration provide services for appointing one or more arbitrators and for the conduct of the proceedings.

In the case of construction contracts, the *Institution of Civil Engineers' Conditions of Contract*, fourth edition, formed the basis of an international edition known as the 'FIDIC' conditions. The third edition of which (at the time of going to Press – October 87) FIDIC dated 1977 is the current version, the fifth edition of ICE (1973) not yet having been generally incorporated into FIDIC.

The ICC will generally appoint a tribunal of three, whilst the London Court will appoint one or more as is appropriate to the dispute, ensuring that the total number of arbitrators is uneven.

The growth of international law and procedures relating to arbitration is fast – the arbitral rules adopted by the General Council of the United Nations in 1976, known as the UNCITRAL (United Nations Committee on International Trade Law) rules, are being incorporated in many contracts and by many arbitral organisations.

One of the reasons for this, apart from the very rapid growth of international trade, is because it is built, so to speak, out of prefabricated elements, and whole sections of English commercial law are thus being internationalised.

International development projects, joint ventures and the like require flexible contractual relationships and these in turn require new kinds of 'legal management', to prevent or resolve dispute situations.

The whole position in relation to 'overseas' arbitration, and in particular the enforceability of Awards, without which the exercise will be completely abortive, is a very encouraging one. Since 1977, UNCITRAL has been developing a 'model law' as the most satisfactory way of harmonising enforcement practices of member States. In 1981 the Secretariat submitted a very comprehensive review of the goals and general principles of what such a law should contain.

This was considered by UNCITRAL in Vienna in 1981 and authority given to proceed. A working group was established which includes the UK, USA, USSR and France amongst the fifteen States represented. This has met twice a year since with some non-governmental representatives which included the ICC, the International Bar Association and the International Law Association.

The principal objectives of the model law are:

1. To liberalise international commercial arbitration by **limiting the role of national courts** to give effect to the 'autonomy of the will' of the parties to choose how their disputes should be determined;
2. To establish a core of mandatory provisions to ensure fairness;
3. To provide a framework for procedure if the parties cannot agree so as to enable the process to be completed;
4. To establish provisions to aid enforceability of Awards.

Progress, by international standards, has been extremely rapid and at time of going to press (autumn 1987) it is expected that the model law will be adopted by the United Nations and promulgated within a year.

It should be noted that what is being developed is a 'model law'. It will then be open to individual States to adopt the law in suitably revised form for their own framework of existing national law.

The model law will not apply to domestic, i.e. internal arbitrations, but is intended to affect international commercial arbitrations held within their territories.

The structure of the model law is:

Scope of application
Arbitration agreement
Arbitration and the courts
Composition of Arbitral Tribunal
Place and conduct of arbitration proceedings
Rules application to substance of dispute
Making of Award and other decisions
Duration of mandate of Arbitral Tribunal
Recognition and enforcement of Award

Articles I and II define the scope, definition of 'international' and 'commercial', which will be illustrated rather than defined. It requires the arbitration agreement to be in writing, but agreements established by telex, etc. are included.

Article III at present states:

In matters governed by this law, no court shall intervene except where so provided in this law.

Later, Article XXV provides for the enforcement of the Award inside the territory in which it was held, Article XXVI for the enforcement outside the State in which it was held, and Article XXX the grounds on which a court can 'rescue' an arbitration to prevent it being a total nullity.

Thus where the model law is adopted parties will be able to have their dispute tried by a tribunal of their choosing; the tribunal will have great flexibility of procedure, but providing these are conducted properly they can then look to the local national court to enforce the Award.

Nominating an Arbitrator in the contract

Some forms of contract allow the nomination of the Arbitrator at the time of signing the contract and prior to any dispute having arisen. This has merit in that immediately a difficulty occurs the Arbitrator is known and he can begin his investigation and determine the dispute at the earliest possible moment. It is also felt that it is better for the parties to know who will deal with their dispute rather than to try to make an appointment when the parties are already in difference and when anything and everything could well be the subject of disagreement, thus making it particularly difficult to agree on a suitable Arbitrator. Equally, they feel the procedure of applying to some other body and going through its appointment procedures is likely to delay the resolution of the difference and is also therefore not desirable.

But there are also disadvantages in naming the Arbitrator in a construction case. Until a difference occurs over a building contract it is not possible to know what area of expertise is required of the Arbitrator. The dispute could arise over failure to proceed or complete part or all of the building on time. This is an organisational matter.

It could be over the cost of the works to date, or at the conclusion, which is essentially a matter of measurement and could be in the field of a quantity surveyor.

Alternatively, it might be a structural failure. But in considering a structural failure is it the result of faulty calculations, and therefore an engineering design matter, or faulty workmanship, or is it the strength of concrete which requires a testing laboratory or, again, might it be a failure of reinforcement as a result of a chemical reaction between reinforcement and the concrete or its cladding?

Again, it may be a question of the failure of a heating or air-conditioning system. This could also be the result of the design or performance of the boiler or heating system, and could in turn be a fault of construction of the plenum chamber or of pressure linings, joints, etc. The fault might also be the result of faulty specification or faulty materials or workmanship.

Then again, the dispute may be over the essential meaning of legal clauses in the contract or in the effect of statutory legislation affecting the contract, in which case a specialist in building law might be the more appropriate Arbitrator.

If such complex matters proceeded to litigation each side would appoint several experts to investigate and present their view of the cause of the trouble. They would each prepare their 'experts' reports and would later argue their case as expert witnesses at any hearing in the court or in an arbitration.

All of this should be borne in mind when considering both the arbitration clause and the appointment of an Arbitrator for a contract which is likely to continue for several years.

In Chapter 8 we will consider this matter further and I will set out some suggestions on ways which will get the best of all worlds for the many who have included arbitration clauses in their contracts but have been loath to use them. But, for those faced with this decision now, some of the appointment forms referred to above illustrate better that the vital first step to get a competent Arbitrator appointed is no more difficult than completing a renewal application for a vehicle licence, and thereafter the right Arbitrator will see that the benefits of the arbitration will result to all parties.

The application forms appropriate to a unilateral or joint appointment of the Chartered Institute of Arbitrators, such as could apply to a construction dispute are shown in Figs 6.1 (a) and (b), together with that relating to a travel dispute under the ABTA scheme which relates essentially to a Hearing on documents only (Fig. 6.1 (c)). The forms used by the RIBA and RICS for similar purposes show an even simpler approach to the preliminary activity (Figs 6.1 (d) – (e)).

THE CHARTERED INSTITUTE OF ARBITRATORS

Registration No:

Unilateral Application for Appointment of an
Arbitrator

IN THE MATTER OF AN ARBITRATION BETWEEN:

CLAIMANT:
    of

AND:

RESPONDENT:
    of

INTERNATIONAL ARBITRATION CENTRE
75 CANNON STREET
LONDON EC4N 5BH
Telephone: 01-236 8761
Telex: 893466 CIARB G

Secretary:
K. R. K. HARDING, MITD, ACIArb

WHEREAS

(1) An Agreement between the above parties dated the   day of   19
    includes provision whereby in the event of a dispute either party may
    apply to the Chartered Institute of Arbitrators to appoint an
    Arbitrator in the matter

(2) Such a dispute has now arisen

(3) Particulars of the said agreement and the said dispute are annexed hereto

(4) Any condition precedent to the right of either party to make Unilateral
    application for the appointment of an Arbitrator has been satisfied and
    particulars (if any) are annexed hereto

NOW THEREFORE I/WE HEREBY APPLY to the Chartered Institute of Arbitrators
to appoint an Arbitrator in accordance with the said Agreement to hear and
determine the said dispute

AND I/WE ENCLOSE HEREWITH the prescribed Registration Fee and I/WE FURTHER
AGREE as a condition of such an appointment:

(i)   To pay the reasonable fees and expenses of the Arbitrator whether or
        not the arbitration reaches a hearing or any Award is made and

ii)   To provide adequate security for such payment if the Arbitrator so
       requests and

(iii)   To make such payment within ten days of receipt of notice that the
       Award is ready to be taken up or that such payment is otherwise due
       and

(iv)   To inform the Arbitrator of the terms of any settlement reached before
       the closing of the hearing so that such terms may be incorporated in
       an Award

SIGNED:

    as, or for and on behalf of, Claimant

DATE:

(UA/1 - 82/7)

Fig. 6.1 (a)–(e)   Arbitrator's appointment forms.

Fig. 6.1 (a) (i)

REQUEST FOR ARBITRATION

Registration No:

CLAIMANT: RESPONDENT:
Name   Name
Address   Address

Tel. No.   Tel. No.

Solicitors/Advisers: Solicitors/Advisers:
Name   Name
Address   Address

Tel. No.   Tel. No.

CONTRACT/AGREEMENT: Date:
(enclose a copy or summarise briefly)

ARBITRATION CLAUSE OR AGREEMENT:
(A copy of this is essential in the case of a Unilateral Application. A
Joint Application may itself be considered an arbitration agreement)

DISPUTE:
(Brief particulars of nature, circumstances and location, of dispute, issue
for arbitration and amount at issue are all that are required at this stage.
The parties will be asked to make detailed submissions in due course.

OTHER RELEVANT DETAILS:

(e.g. unilateral application: date on which other party was requested to
concur in appointment of arbitrator, names of arbitrators proposed etc.
joint application: matters on which parties have agreed regarding conduct
of the arbitration etc.)

(UA/JA/2 - 82/7)

Fig. 6.1 (a) (ii)

THE CHARTERED INSTITUTE OF ARBITRATORS

Registration No:

Joint Application for the Appointment of an
Arbitrator

IN THE MATTER OF AN ARBITRATION BETWEEN:

INTERNATIONAL ARBITRATION CENTRE
75 CANNON STREET
LONDON EC4N 5BH
Telephone: 01-236 8761
Telex: 893466 CIARB G

Secretary:
K. R. K. HARDING, MITD, ACIArb

CLAIMANT:
    of

AND:

RESPONDENT:
    of

WE HEREBY APPLY to the Chartered Institute of Arbitrators to appoint an
Arbitrator in a dispute between us particulars of which are annexed hereto

AND WE HEREBY REFER the said dispute to such Arbitrator to hear and
determine the same in accordance with the Arbitration Acts 1950 to 1979 and
any statutory modification thereof for the time being in force and with the
Chartered Institute of Arbitrators Arbitration Rules 1981

AND WE ENCLOSE HEREWITH the prescribed Registration Fee

Signed:

    as, or for an on behalf of, Claimant

DATE:

Signed:

    as, or for and on behalf of, Respondent

DATE:

(JA/1 - 82/7)

Fig. 6.1 (b)

THE CHARTERED INSTITUTE OF ARBITRATORS

Arbitration Scheme for the Association of British Travel Agents

APPLICATION FOR ARBITRATION

To: The Chartered Institute of Arbitrators
(To be submitted through:
Association of British Travel Agents
55 Newman Street, London W1P 4AH)

ABTA REF. NO.

CI Arb REF NO. 5/ABTA/

1 _____ **Claimant**
(Customer)

of (permanent address): _____

_____(Phone _____)

    Address for Claimant's correspondence (if different from above):

    _____

    _____

    _____(Phone _____)

AND

_____ **Respondent**
(Tour Operator)

of _____

_____(Phone _____)

hereby apply to the Chartered Institute of Arbitrators for the following dispute to be referred to arbitration under the rules of the Scheme for determination by an arbitrator appointed for that purpose by the Institute.

2 The dispute has arisen in connection with the following inclusive holiday booking which was made in _____(date):

    Holiday location:

    Holiday dates: Departure _____ Return _____

    Total cost of holiday: £ _____
    (ie, the amount paid to the Tour Operator)

3 Compensation is claimed in the total sum of £ _____ the claim being made in respect of the following persons (*age and relationship may be relevant to registration fees in 4 below):

NAMES in block letters (include Claimant in 1 above)	*AGE at date of booking if under 12	*RELATIONSHIP to Claimant in 1 above
(1)		
(2)		
(3)		
(4)		
(5)		
(6)		

Fig. 6.1 (b) (ii)

Royal Institute of British Architects, 66 Portland Place, London W1N 4AD

Appointment of an Arbitrator

Note: This form is to be used where the dispute arises under a building contract or other agreement wherein there is provision for arbitration.
A/B

Regarding the agreement dated the _____ day of _____ and made

between _____ of the one part

and _____ of the other part and where there
is a submission to arbitration, within the meaning of the Arbitration Act 1950,
of any dispute or difference which shall arise between the parties.

WHEREAS a dispute or difference has arisen in connection therewith

I / We hereby ask the President of the Royal Institute of British Architects to appoint an arbitrator to hear and determine the matter.

As a Condition of the Appointment I / We jointly and severally agree as follows:

(1) To provide adequate security for the due payment of the fees and expenses of the Arbitrator if he so requires.

(2) To pay the fees and expenses of the Arbitrator whether the Arbitration reaches a Hearing or not.

(3) To take up the Award (if any) within ten days from receipt of notice of publication.

(Signed) _____

of _____

_____

(Signed) _____

of _____

_____

Dated this _____ day of _____ 19 _____

I hereby appoint _____

of _____

_____

Arbitrator in the above matter.

(Signed) _____

President of the Royal Institute of British Architects

Dated this _____ day of _____ 19 _____

I hereby accept the appointment of Arbitrator in the above matter.

(Signed) _____

8.87   Dated this _____ day of _____ 19 _____

Fig. 6.1 (c)

SPECIMEN

THE PRESIDENT'S OFFICE
THE ROYAL INSTITUTION OF CHARTERED SURVEYORS
12, GREAT GEORGE STREET, PARLIAMENT SQUARE
WESTMINSTER, SW1P 3AD

01-222 7000

I, [name of President], President of the Royal Institution of Chartered Surveyors, hereby appoint

[name, qualifications and address
  of arbitrator]

as   Arbitrator

to determine a dispute between

[name and address of Claimant]   Claimant

and

[name and address of Respondent]   Respondent

concerning works carried out at [address of premises].

This appointment is made in accordance with Clause 27 of the sub-contract relating to the said works made between the Claimant and the Respondent and dated ....

                                 (signed)
Dated this ....
                                 President

Ref No:

Fig. 6.1 (d)

PART III

PREVENTION AND CURE

CHAPTER 7

PREVENTING DISPUTES – MANAGEMENT PROCEDURES AND PRACTICES

Good project management procedures that will go a long way to preventing disputes are set out for the client and the design team and illustrated by reference to case studies of disputes emanating from the client area, and that of the design team.

The purpose of the contract documents in identifying the promises made by the various parties which they intend to be legally binding and the communications or arrangements which are made in various other documents are examined, and the importance of their consistency with each other is stressed.

The implications of subcontract arrangements are identified in relation to the dispute potential.

Steps that should be taken by all parties to ensure lines of communication coincide with lines of contract and the importance of an overall Procedure Manual as a dispute-prevention and document-co-ordination device are set out, together with illustrations of successful practices.

Action that the contractor can take upon his appointment if the measures necessary have not already been taken are given, showing how adjudication concepts are the logical and practical outcome of the better project management procedures.

Chapter 4 examined management principles bearing on disputes in the Construction Industry. But prevention is better than cure and good management is the preventive medicine of dispute.

The *RIBA Management Handbook* defined management as 'the creation of conditions to bring about the optimum use of all resources available to an undertaking in men, methods and materials'. If we now consider the undertaking as being a large building project, say an opera house or a large Head Office from an international corporation, then the responsibility for establishing these good management procedures rests successively in different hands:

A. Initially, those of the client – for establishing the brief and determining the basic organisation structure for execution of the project.
B. For the design – the design team leader, be he architect or engineer.
C. For the construction – the contractor's project manager or agent.

A. Client-orientated problems

Undoubtedly many construction disputes have their origin in the seeds sown by, or in, the client's area. Two recent cases illustrate this quite clearly.

Case Study 1: Dispute in Head Office

This dispute resulted primarily from the take-over of the client, a financial institution, by another during the course of construction of its Head Office.

Work started on site in 1972, the architect never issued a final certificate, but litigation was started in 1979 although disputes over various matters had been going on since 1977.

The claim was for negligence in the amount of £1.6 million plus interest against seven defendants: the architects, two consulting mechanical and electrical engineers, the mechanical and electrical design contractor who succeeded them, the consulting structural engineers, the main contractor, and a window manufacturer.

The matter was settled before going into court in 1983, by which time 18 'experts' had totalled around 8,000 hours at a cost of say £300,000, and there was an enormous (and unnecessary) volume of documentation. The points of claim took 7 thick volumes, with another 2 volumes of detailed complaints and 4 sets of addenda. There were 6 firms of lawyers and 9 legal counsel involved preparing the case for court.

Undoubtedly the building was defective, but the question was whether and to what extent any of the seven defendant firms were negligent.

The cost of the experts and lawyers before settlement came to about £1 million on top of the £1.6 million claimed in the main action.

Of course, there were many areas where error, mismanagement, confusion and perhaps some degree of negligence (in the legal sense at any rate) were spread around the various contractors.

But undoubtedly, the confused pattern of client communications, sometimes perhaps deliberate, sometimes inevitable, resulted from changes at the top of the corporation as a result of the change-over, and subsequent changes in the client's command structure were all major factors in the problems that arose.

A major factor, too, were the different expectations of the new bosses against the original 'brief' settled (well, partly settled) by the old guard. The new management were only too pleased to have the problems with the building illustrate the inadequacies of the old management and then to apply their own standards, or even attitudes without predefined standards, without studying the original brief. The brief had been drawn up, however adequately or inadequately, within a culture different from that of the corporation 'taking over'. The building team undoubtedly suffered, probably because no one involved really appreciated what was happening and did not take firm enough measures to prevent the problems affecting the project.

Case Study 2

The second case, a new Head Office building for an international corporation, was built by developers and involved a dispute between the international bank who financed the development group, the company whose headquarters it was intended to be, the original developers, the general contractor who carried out the main construction work, the subcontractor for mechanical, electrical and flooring works, the architect, the consulting structural engineer and the consulting mechanical and electrical engineers.

Work started on site in 1974 and the eventual litigation began in 1980 and was settled in 1983.

When the case reached the formal dispute stage there were 10 firms of lawyers, plus 5 leading and 10 junior counsel, and the following 'experts': 2 firms of surveyors and valuers, 3 quantity surveying firms, 5 consulting engineers, and half a dozen other experts. The original building contract in 1974 was just over £5 million. The action brought by the international bank against 9 different firms in 1978 was over £2 million plus interest. It is probable that the total bill for the professionals involved in the dispute was not much less. One of the experts alone, with a relatively small involvement, incurred fees for 240 hours at around £12,000!

Here again, the real cause of the problems was the confused situation which came about in the client's area when there was a change in the world's financial confidence, and a business recession took place.

Lack of a sound project management structure resulted in a piecemeal approach to the project under construction by several groups within the various client organisations.

Undoubtedly the biggest need after defining the brief within the organisation is for the client to establish a single project organisation structure and to define within this the role and responsibilities of the main 'players' and then to ensure that the lines of contract and lines of communication coincide. This must start with identifying his own 'client' responsibilities.

An English proverb says: 'Well begun is half done.'

Well begun in the context of a multi-disciplinary construction project can be identified by extending the mnemonic for the client's brief in Fig. 4.3 – FACT – adding 'OPLAN' to create a code word FACTOPLAN identifying all the components that should be considered before instructing any work on the project by outside agencies or firms – no matter how expert.

Appointment of client representative

The most important project appointment is that of 'the client man' or 'client representative'. He should be seen as **the** single representative of the client through whom **all** instructions are issued, by whom all communications are received and whose authority, responsibilities and accountabilities have been clearly defined.

Every architect and consulting engineer, and every contractor, knows that 'the client' is never one person but too frequently is seen as a 'many-headed-beast', all of whom have been known to issue directives, take an interest, make complaints, but only very rarely to speak with one voice, and then only when it is to disclaim responsibility for causing delay, requiring extensions of time, or additional cost to be added to the contract sum. The appointment of 'client representative' will do much to ensure a successful project providing the right man is appointed and given the time and authority to carry out his task.

Who should it be?

It could be almost any executive in the client's organisation, providing he has the competence – or someone appointed specifically for this purpose from the outside providing he understands the client's operations, and if he understands Construction as well so much the better.

But, the client man should **never** be the client's managing director or chief executive officer. Preferably the client man should report direct to him, or to the Board, and if of sufficient seniority and experience he should have delegated powers for a wide spectrum of functional project operating and cost decisions.

Defining the brief

As discussed in Chapter 4, the client man's first task should be to prepare a programme for the first phase of the project – getting the brief.

The brief should consist of a definition or general description of the client's needs or wants under the headings:

F Function. All the technical and physical performance requirements for the project/building.

A Aesthetic. Including social and human factors relating to the development.

C Cost implications. Perhaps bracketing upper and lower limits overall and for any particular variations of quality for various parts of the scheme and for the first (capital) cost related to 'cost in use' (running costs).

T Time. For completion overall and then any particular phases or stages if these are to come into operation earlier.

In expressing these 'FACTS' one at least of the various requirements must be 'open-ended' or the emphasis or priority to be given should always be stated – for example, to time versus cost, or function versus cost, or function and cost-in-use.

The second part of the keyword – 'OPLAN' – might come a little later when the requirements of the client have been considered in terms of practical construction methods and after an initial design conception or alternative possibilities have emerged:

O Organisation. Developing a control system, defining responsibilities, establishing relationships of various client executives to the project and to the design team. This should have already been set up with or by the client man but will need continually developing and updating as consultants, designers, contractors and sub-contractors or suppliers are chosen.

P Planning. The setting of time and cost objectives. Establishing procedures, budgets, schedules, tasks for the various people involved. This will sometimes need to be done by the client man but at other times these tasks will be delegated (and by the terms of the various contracts of appointment) to the architect, engineer or others.

Throughout the period from conception to completion of the project the communication channels and relationships of people (perhaps both by name and functional title) will need to be established, maintained and updated in order that effective

L Liaison takes place.

Perhaps the most effective way of dealing with all of these matters of responsibility, relationships, communication, scheduling and controlling is to

A Activate by the preparation of a

N Network analysis diagram – in one or more of its various forms, e.g.

critical path planning (CPM), resource allocation and multi-project scheduling (RAMPS), – program evaluation and review technique (PERT), etc.

This approach will ensure that the project will get off along the right path – critical or not – but it is no guarantee that problems will not arise later.

No large organisation big enough to undertake capital projects running into millions of pounds is 'static'. It is a living organism of people who are themselves seeking a variety of objectives – some corporate and others personal.

During the course of a large capital project these seemingly background influences can change, and exert extraordinary pressures upon a project. The two case studies illustrate this only too expensively, particularly for all those involved 'downstream' on the project, and that means virtually everyone in the Construction Industry!

B. Management responsibilities during the design stage

Let us now look at the management responsibilities and what can be done about improving them at the next stage in the evolution of the project from the point of view of:

(a) the design team;
(b) Specialists who become subcontractors responsible for the execution of particular parts of the works.

To do this let us first discuss the legal relationships and promises these parties have made and then how in practice they should organise themselves to minimise the problems and pitfalls that the various contracts could otherwise provide for them.

The principal contracting parties to the construction contract are 'the employer' (or building owner) and the 'general contractor' who undertakes to provide for the project's every (?) need.

The law of contract within which the particular project contract is signed is concerned above all else with enforceable promises. That is to say, statements the parties make about their future actions and make in accordance with the appropriate rituals of the law, with the intention that the law will legally enforce what they promised to do.

It is obvious that contractual promises are not the only sort of promises; many statements about future conduct are neither intended to be subject to the law, nor indeed is it possible to make them so. However, it is plain that some degree of sanction must be applied where highly complex human organisations are involved, with their multiplicity of interrelating promises. All these promises, when performed, add up to the building.

Organisational technology in building has always been a complicated matter, but in very crude terms we can distinguish the following sequence of happenings:

1. Decide upon the project (e.g. a theatre, concert hall complex, etc.).
2. Set up an organisation of people whose skill and experience will be necessary (e.g. designers, stonemasons, plumbers, sound engineers, curtain manufacturers, etc.).
3. Formulate the promises which each of the persons have to make (e.g. to design, to supervise, to advise, to build).
4. Performance of all the duties.
5. In the event of broken promises or failures of the organisation, to remedy the failures by legal process.

In real life, of course, the organisation is to some extent a 'standing' one. Each project must have its own organisation created, *ad hoc*, for the purpose by the appointment of individuals to the various positions in the structure but, in practice, the skeleton of the organisation is already there in the firms who offer to undertake the parts of the project, and each man knows, or thinks he knows, what part he has to play and merely has to step into it. The details of the organisation are very largely the result of tradition and common practice. These have changed surprisingly little in the twentieth century.

But the one who usually does not know the ropes and for whom membership of the organisation is a completely new experience is the building owner – or employer as he is called in contracts. He steps into a position of great responsibility without really being aware of what he is letting himself in for.

It has long been the custom for such an employer to hire a man who does know the ropes to act for him, as his agent, in the affair. This agent's work, which has come to be called project management, is quite distinct from that of designing buildings and supervising their construction. This work of project management is traditionally done by 'the architect' or 'the engineer'. But in practice, on a large project 'the architect' is, in fact, a number of people, some of whom earn their bread by project management, others by designing, some broadly, others in detail, and others by specifying and supervising the works.

It is noteworthy that the Code of Conduct to which a British architect must adhere requires that he:

> take the earliest opportunity to explain to his client the conditions of the Contract.

This is not an easy duty to perform, but it is a fundamental one. Communication in simple and intelligible terms of the promises made by all the people in the project organisation is a necessary preliminary to the building owner's understanding of the part he must play.

A building contract – the piece of paper on which a lot of lawyer's magic is written – can be regarded in one of two ways.

First, it can be seen as a word picture of the organisation and a detailed list of promises. This word picture is obviously a document of communication. It is a criticism of building contracts that they do not communicate to the uninitiated. All that can be said is that they are generally not as bad as some other legal documents but the communication could be very much improved.

Second, the contracts can be regarded in litigation as a message to 'the judge' to assist him in his work, which is that of establishing the rights and duties of the parties. Plainly, this aspect is a very different one from the first. It is concerned primarily with failure rather than with success, and it ought to be remembered that with building contracts, as with most promises made in this world, success is infinitely more frequent than failure. It is the failure that makes the headlines. But an over-emphasis on this aspect has resulted in a neglect of the former and there are ways in which it may now be improved.

There are many 'standard forms of contract' having their own conventions, history and usage. The essential points of principle in the standard forms are:

1. They are the contract between two parties, the employer and the contractor. The latter promises to build, the former to pay.
2. Generally the rules of law do not admit of rights or liabilities being created in respect of third parties who are not privy to this contract.
3. Therefore, the other promises (such as that between a consultant and the employer) have to be dealt with in other contracts.

Perhaps the most important aspect and the one most abused in practice is to:

4. Ensure that all of the contracts are consistent with each other and, even more important.
5. Ensure that the standard 'legal' form is only one of the main documents, instructions and information that already exist and which with others that will come along later will comprise the complete documentary system for carrying out the project.

Failure to make up a complete set of clear promises will result in expensive trouble when almost anything unforeseen occurs on site.

In the JCT forms of contract, the Employer sets up the Architect or Engineer as his Agent and defines the scope of that agent's authority. In general terms this is as follows:

1. To give instructions in regard to variation or modification of the work contracted for.
2. To condemn work or materials not up to the standard required.

3. To give instructions on the postponement of any work.
4. To require dismissal of inadequate persons employed upon the work.
5. To give instructions regarding defects.

In general these powers are of a fairly limited nature. Some standard forms recognise that, in practice, an architect may, inadvertently, give instructions for which he has no authority, and a provision is included to deal with this situation. The contractor may require the architect to show where he gets his authority and there are generally also provisions for arbitration in the event of a dispute.

But any complex project requires both specialist designers and subcontractors to carry out some of the work within the main contract. Most standard contract forms provide for these services to be provided by "nominated" subcontractors and suppliers.

Put into very simple terms, this means that the Employer has the right to interfere with the contractor's conduct of the work to the extent of telling the contractor the names of those whom he wishes to subcontract for certain declared operations. It should be noted that the contractor is entitled to refuse such nominations, but in practice this is not often done. The object of all this is an attempt to get the best of both worlds: (a) to leave the contractor all the risks of dealing with a subcontractor, and leave intact his responsibility for management of the subcontract and dealing with the money; and (b) at the same time to obtain some control by the employer over the people, or rather the choice of the people, who are to carry out specialist works.

This system does in fact deal with the numerous matters where accurate specification of work is almost impossible. Cases like this, where reliance must be placed upon the known abilities of specialist subcontractors, cannot be left merely to the contractor to tender for, using the lowest prices he can obtain. For example, the installation of highly complex and sophisticated electric equipment in a theatre is a matter where the employer and his advisers have probably spent months or even years negotiating with a given manufacturer. They cannot merely specify what they want and leave it to the contractor to obtain tenders.

On the other hand, it can reasonably be argued that the procedure necessary to give legal effect to arrangements of this kind is so exceedingly complex and requires so much knowledge of law and practice that it is a near impossibility for those who have to deal with such matters from day to day to understand fully what they are about. It is not surprising, therefore, that a great proportion of the troubles that do arise in building come from this source.

The theory is that the contractor's right and duty to manage the works in their entirety is left unimpaired but, in practice, this beautifully simple conception frequently does not work out.

To establish a good project management system it is important that the employer and the design team and subcontractors understand the contracts they are signing and then see that their operational practices and relationship are consistent with their contractual promises, and relationships.

Case Study 3 Design-team failures affecting construction

To illustrate what can go wrong on a project if these relationships are not properly considered let me refer to a case where it seemed that everything that could go wrong, did, and other factors that few would have expected then added to the chaos.

Figure 7.1(a) shows what the relationships were at the time I was called into investigate – although it did take some time to establish, as many of the firms and people involved found it difficult to say who was reporting to whom operationally!

The project had started well enough. A management consultant had carried out an initial study on the client's existing plant, which was concerned with manufacturing chemicals. As a result of this a chemical consultant had been retained to design the new and much enlarged process plant for which a 'greenfield' site some 10 miles away had been selected.

The client also appointed his chief chemist, a bright keen man in his early thirties, to be 'his representative' for all meetings with the chemical consultants and later, when they were appointed, with the architects, an internationally known firm, and the quantity surveyors, who were well known in the UK although neither, it seemed, had a great deal of experience in the Greater London area where the project was sited.

The building contract which had been negotiated was said to be a 'lump-sum-fixed-price' contract with approximate bills of quantity to be completed in 52 weeks with most of the process plant work let on individual contracts by the chemical consultants. A further 26 weeks had been allowed for the completion of the process plant after the practical completion of the building contract so that production on the new site was expected to commence in phases 18 months to 2 years after work had commenced there, whilst production was run down over the same period as the existing works closed and was demolished as part of a general local authority redevelopment of the area.

After several months, during which the client, a public company, had continually expressed its concern both over the lack of progress and the general conduct of the works and the workmanship under the building contract to the architect, the quantity surveyor, the builder, and generally to anyone who would listen, the author was called in in week 70 to 'trouble-shoot' the project with the client's priorities stated as:

1. Establish what needed to be done for earliest practical completion.

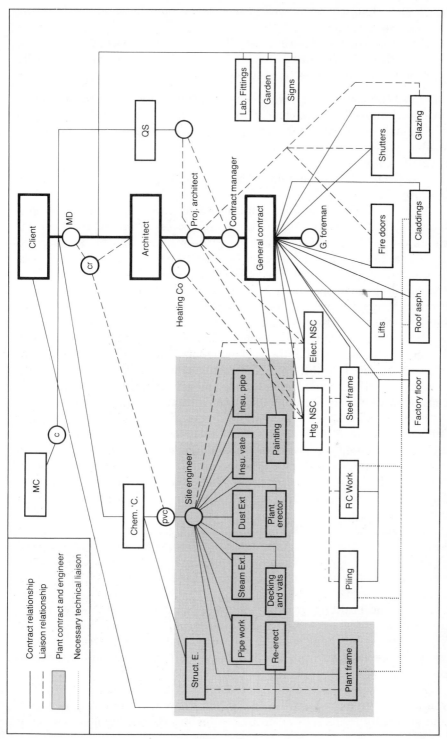

Fig. 7.1 Contract organisation structure. **(a)** Relationships as existing in Week 40 – Case Study 3.

2. Ensure that whatever was needed to be done was put in train by those responsible.
3. Report on the relative responsibilities of those concerned (there were some thirty major firms involved), and what, if anything, could be done to obtain redress from those who were responsible.

At that time construction work was approximately half finished, much poor workmanship could clearly be seen, a man had been killed on the site, morale was extremely low, progress, due to 2 or 3 weeks of bad winter weather, was virtually nil, and the architect asked to attend a specially called Board Meeting of the client company had failed to turn up – saying he had been delayed by the opening of one of his buildings by a royal personage!

Apart from the relatively self-contained office, laboratory and canteen blocks, the construction of the main process plant required careful co-ordination, not only because the process plant was to be installed during weeks 36 to 52 but also because the process equipment was suspended in several levels of steel frame independent of, but within, the building envelope, both building and plant frame came down to common ground beams sitting on short-bored piles, the whole site once having been marshland adjoining a river!

My first quick appraisal – aimed at getting anything that needed to be done in the way of planning – placing forward orders, giving notice of starting dates for installation of subcontractors' work, etc. showed up a remarkable difference in both attitude and administration by the 'client's representative' and their chemical consultants on the one hand, and with one notable exception, virtually everyone connected with the building works on the other.

Both the client's representative and the chemical consultants had excellent written records of all the meetings they had attended, instructions they had given, questions they had asked, apprehensions they had felt, and even fears they had expressed to the architect and the general contractor.

However, they had both known that they were not experienced in this kind of building operation, and had therefore given way, or not pressed their 'amateur' status when given explanations or 'reasons' by the building 'team'. 'Don't worry, it will be all right on the night' was their recurring attitude.

As for the building group, here the general attitude was 'Well, it's always like this, isn't it?' 'It will all be sorted out at the final account. Then when the client has his building and he is getting on with increased production from his new factory all the problems will disappear, etc.'

Surprise was even expressed at 'the fuss you are making – after all you are not green behind the ears – you know what building is like' – and generally there seemed to be the feeling that everyone was doing his best – even working hard – and why should anyone be concerned, building was like this, only clients and people who did not know anything about building would expect anything different!

The job administration – files, records of meetings, amendments to drawings, of which there were many – and documentation generally was in a poor state, where it existed at all, and to crown it all, the signed copies of 'the contract drawings' had huge 'deletions' written on by the quantity surveyor and the (RIBA) form of contract was not stamped!

Many management lessons could be learned from a depth study of this project that went wrong – but certainly there is no doubt that had a **Project Manual of Management Responsibilities** been established during the design stage many, if not all, the problems which arose would have been dealt with and a great deal more quickly and cheaply.

Certainly the muddle, organisationally, which developed through the lack of clear delegation would have been avoided. Figure 7.1 (b) shows the structure which could have been created during the design stages – each position being accompanied by a written description in the manual (see pages 122–3) – Fig. 7.1 (c) shows how this could have been amended when the building contract was signed. I emphasise 'could', for there can be many organisational solutions – what is important is that the structure receives consideration and definition reflecting the various firms involved and the philosophy behind the structural organisation. It is certainly as important, if not as time-consuming, as that which is given to the construction of the load-bearing frame of the building by a structural engineer.

The structural formulae and component strength for each member in the framework are as yet still difficult to define. For these are human structures whose behaviour, as we have seen from the study of the work of Maslow and McGregor, is the result of many influences and motivations. But, the case history set out here shows how the failure to analyse the *need* resulted in a complete structural failure of the organisation. It is not easy to assess the cost of this failure, nor is it necessary for my purpose to try, but the reader might not forgive me if I did not summarise the outcome, at least in general terms.

Outcome and settlement

My first report, in week 80, recommended that no contracts should be terminated and that all things necessary to be done, had by then been done. This I felt would be less disturbing to completion and final settlement. I also felt that as I was 'looking over their shoulders' so to speak, proper attention would be given in the future. In this, however, I was wrong.

The project architect, perhaps in a rut, or perhaps because he, his senior partner, and the whole firm were 'overworked' (for which I would

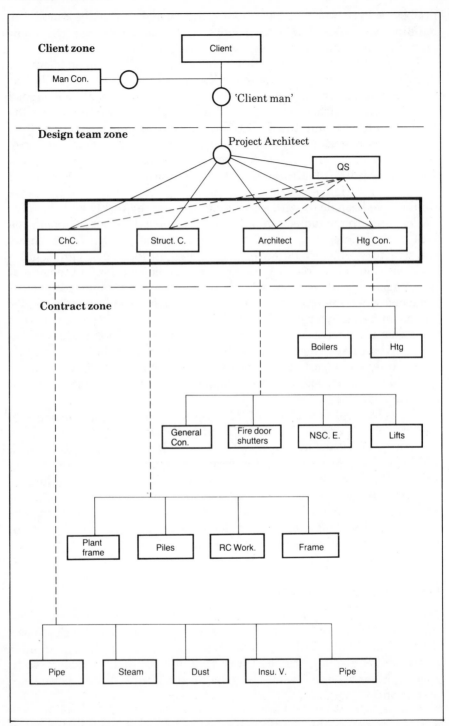

Fig. 7.1 (b) Project relationship Improved Structure – Design Phase.

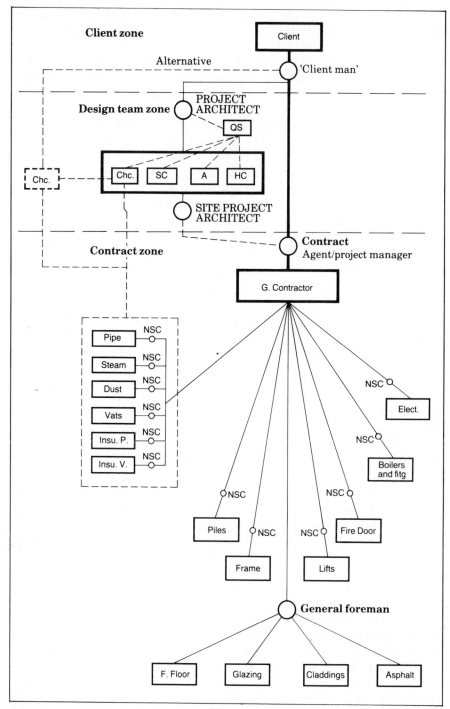

Fig. 7.1 (c) Project structure, construction phase. Relationships to overcome and control difficulties.

prefer to substitute 'badly managed') did not mend their ways and the contractor continued to take his cue from the architect with whom he had negotiated the contract.

At any event, in about week 80 the building owner, looking ahead to the date when he was committed to leaving his existing factory, and saw liquidation staring him in the face when he failed to fulfil production commitments, changed my terms of reference.

A new architect was appointed and I assumed some of the responsibilities as project manager, but not interfering in the duties of the new architect named under the existing building contract which continued with the existing contractor and his various subcontractors — some of whom were also responsible for parts of the design.

The building works took a further 30–40 weeks. Notionally, completion was certified at the end of week 97 but it is difficult to say just when practical completion took place as remedial work was involved and continued throughout the 6 months maintenance period up to week 129. But the building owner did manage, at considerable extra cost to himself and to some of the process plant contractors, to get into production in time to save his supply commitments – and to get out of his old works in time to satisfy a renegotiated date with the local authority!

The new architect refused to sign a final certificate, saying he was not happy with what he had seen since taking over and he certainly was not going to say that he was with what had gone on before he took over. The contractor notified (to put it mildly!) his intention to arbitrate under the contract and so instructed his solicitors. The building owner, in response, instructed his, and proofs of evidence from all and sundry began to be prepared.

At this stage my quasi-role of 'project manager' became that of conciliator or mediator between the client and the contractor and with the original architect, and quantity surveyors. As a result of these activities and with the support from the contemporary records of the 'amateur' chemical consultants and 'client representative' as the best supplementary evidence available to support the contractual muddle of amended contract drawings, unstamped memorandum of agreement, approximate (and largely unpriced) bills of quantity, inadequate or non-existent minutes of site meetings, etc. formal arbitration in accordance with the contract did *not* take place.

Instead, settlement was made with the architect that no further action would be taken against him, but no fees beyond those he had already received would be paid. This was virtually the full element for supervision and any extras and disbursements which he may have been due. He was probably well out of it on these terms.

The quantity surveyor received the full fee originally agreed on the original contract sum, but measured and priced both the works of variation and the substantial remedial works. Whilst not admitting that anything that had taken place on the contract had been either his fault or responsibility (nor probably had it), he did not express any dissatisfaction with the outcome either on his own account or with the settlement with the contractor. In the course of the negotiations with the quantity surveyor it appeared that at the request of the architect, with whom he worked frequently, he had carried out some of the work on the specification and drawings, included in the architect's fee, but that was agreed as a matter clearly between him and the architect.

Prior to the appointment of the 'new' architect, certain variations and extras, including some extensions of time for exceptionally inclement weather – although not at that time specified as such – and also for delay in the issue of instructions by the architect – had been agreed with the contractor.

At the time of agreeing the final account these matters were re-examined by the new architect in conjunction with me in my role of quasi-project manager and mediator – a role very similar to that set out in the following chapters for an 'Adjudicator', but in this instance not as a result of a joint appointment.

As a consequence, some of these extras were allowed to stand and some further extensions of time were given amounting in all to 10.5 weeks, mostly for delay in issue of instructions. Some of the extras previously agreed were now included in the remedial works which the contractor was required to do at his own expense and the contractor was paid a final sum approximately 13 per cent higher than the original 'lump-sum fixed-price-contract' sum. Although even after full explanation the client company could not understand why! The client also deducted damages at the agreed rates for 34.5 weeks for non-completion. The contractor never received a final certificate and he too was probably better off than if he had proceeded to the formal arbitration of which he had given notice of intent.

The contractor was probably also entitled to reclaim a sum equal to about 7 per cent of the original contract sum for work he carried out under the first' architect's instructions to comply with statutory conditions which, because of the nature of the various contracts which made the contractor responsible for the design of items to satisfy those requirements, he could not recover from the building owner. He could reasonably have expected the architect in this situation to have provided for these matters, and so could have recovered this from the architect. I do not know whether he did, but I suspect he did not, at least directly.

Just before the end of the first year of work on the site and when things were clearly in a most unsatisfactory state the managing director of the client company had a severe heart attack, and shortly after, the company's shares fell dramatically on the London Stock Exchange.

He eventually recovered and seemed at the time of my appointment in week 70 to be handicapped but reasonably competent, although only working half-time. However, his Board and executive colleagues, who had known him over many years during which he had been largely responsible for the success of the company, said that he was never the same man again. The company also had to meet the cost of my fees and some extra for the new architect, although this was to some extent offset by the fee not paid to the architect whose services were terminated.

The company have continued to prosper in their new factory, the second architect was retained to build an extension, but no one involved in the original project was satisfied with the outcome – and all involved suffered in both financial and human terms.

Corrective procedures

The cost of preparing a Project Manual of Responsibilities and Procedures (Quality Assurance Manuals) is a small price to pay – if indeed it does not actually reduce operating costs as a normal result – on every large contract. On a small one, the time spent will not be great and will still pay for itself in good relations and communications!

All the foregoing emphasise that the biggest area for improvement in project management is a reduction in the incidence and scale of contractual dispute by ensuring that lines of communication and contract coincide and that all contractual communications flow along the established lines of communication and reach all those who should receive them, either for action or just information.

This will require the production of another set of documents, a Project Operations and Procedure Manual, in which is set out the structure, organisational and functional roles and relationships, and the duties and responsibilities of those people filling the various functional roles.

It is of vital importance that the structure and responsibilities are consistent with the contractual 'promises'. The names of the people currently filling each role should be established at an early stage and then maintained.

The extracts which follow illustrate the framework of such a Management Manual as was developed for a recently completed civic theatre project. It therefore deals with 'actual' rather than model or theoretical situations. The principles are, however, clear.

Define the organisation structure and individual responsibilities

The purpose of the various documents contained in the Project Operations Manual is to provide the framework for operations and bring together the responsibilities of the various people involved in the management of the project. The Operations Manual therefore embraces the other documents involved in the project, i.e.:

- The standard form of contract;
- Any documents used for tendering purposes, such as:
- Specification of the works;
- Bill of quantities;
- Programme schedules; and
- Construction drawings.

If a network analysis or critical path plan has been developed then it should have been related to these project-management responsibilities. To a considerable extent the network will develop the relationships and responsibilities in a time sequence, and any network developed should have this project-management structure and relationship appended to it.

The Project Operations and Procedures Manual should be set up and indexed even before it is known just which functions will eventually be involved in design, and certainly before it is known who will perform those functions. Therefore, whilst the index to the manual should be set out at the commencement each section should leave space for additional job functions or paperwork procedures that might be developed (Fig. 7.2).

Overall, it must always be remembered that the lines of contract, as indicated by Fig. 7.3(a) must always be directly reflected in the lines of management responsibility illustrated in Fig. 7.3(b). The management structure which should be created during the design phase should provide the foundation of the organisation for later supervision of the construction team.

Figure 7.3(c) illustrates the danger that exists in large projects where some of the parties fulfil dual roles or whose functional or contractual relationships change at different stages in the project. In this case the theatre consultants who were responsible directly to the client for advising him on the formulation of the technical parts of the brief relating to theatre functions at the later design stages will become responsible to the architect for proper design solutions that both fulfil the client's brief (which they themselves had written) and the spatial, visual and other requirements of the design as conceived by the architect.

Any firm which finds itself with a dual role, and this is a regular rather than an extreme situation, must be doubly careful to fulfil both responsibilities and to remember to 'change hats' and not wear both at the same time!

After the organisation structure has been established each individual's mandate should be set out. In addition to each individual's mandate the design and construction stages are developed and controlled sometimes not by individuals but by 'meetings' (not committees).

The function of these meetings and their constitution should also be set out. Thus the manual sets out for each individual how and where he fits into the total operation.

TYPICAL CIVIC THEATRE   PROJECT OPERATIONS & PROCEDURES MANUAL

INDEX TO MANUAL

PART 1 - PROJECT ORGANISATION STRUCTURE AND RELATIONSHIPS

       - INTRODUCTION
       - DIAGRAMS - A) NEXUS OF CONTRACTS
                   B) PROJECT ORGANISATION - RIBA STAGES A-B
                   C) PROJECT ORGANISATION - RIBA STAGES C-G
                   D) CONSTRUCTION ORGANISATION - RIBA STAGE H

PART 2 - FUNCTION OF MEETINGS DURING CONSTRUCTION PHASE

       I)   ARCHITECT'S SITE MEETING
       II) QUANTITY SURVEYOR'S SITE MEETING
       III) CONTRACTOR'S SITE MEETING
       IV) DESIGN TEAM MEETING - FULL TEAM-ROUTINE
                             - AD HOC

PART 3 - PROJECT MANDATES

              * CLIENT'S REPRESENTATIVE   - (STATE NAME   )
              * PROJECT MANAGER   - (OF CURRENT)
              * JOB ARCHITECT   - (PERSON   )
              ARCHITECT'S DESIGN TEAM TEAM LEADER - (   )
              CLERK OF WORKS   - (   )

      CONSULTANTS * STRUCTURES DESIGNER   - (   )
                MECHANICAL SERVICES DESIGNER   - (   )
                ELECTRICAL SERVICES DESIGNER   - (   )
                THEATRE MANAGEMENT (SERVICES) DESIGNER (   )
                ACOUSTIC SPECIALIST   - (   )
      QUANTITY
      SURVEYOR   CONTRACT VALUATION SURVEYOR   - (   )

      GENERAL   CONTRACT MANAGER   - (   )
      CONTRACTOR   SITE MANAGER   - (   )

      SUB-CONTRACTOR CONTRACT MANAGER   - (   )

PART 4 *PAPERWORK AND FORMAL RECORDING PROCEDURES

       I)   MINUTES OF MEETINGS - DESIGN TEAM
                              - ARCHITECT'S SITE
                              - (NOTE: CONTRACTOR'S MEETINGS WILL BE DETERMINED
                                  AFTER CONTRACTOR APPOINTED)
       II) CLERK OF WORKS WEEKLY REPORT
       III) CLERK OF WORKS DIRECTIONS (RESIDENT ENGINEER'S DIRECTIONS)
       IV) ARCHITECT'S INSTRUCTIONS
       V) ADVICE OF CONTRACT VARIATION
       VI) CONTRACTOR'S QUARTERLY REPORT (TO CLIENT DIRECT)

PART 5 PROJECT DIRECTORY - ADDRESSES/TELEPHONE NOS./ETC.

Fig. 7.2 Index to loose leaf project operations manual.

    * Mandate follows

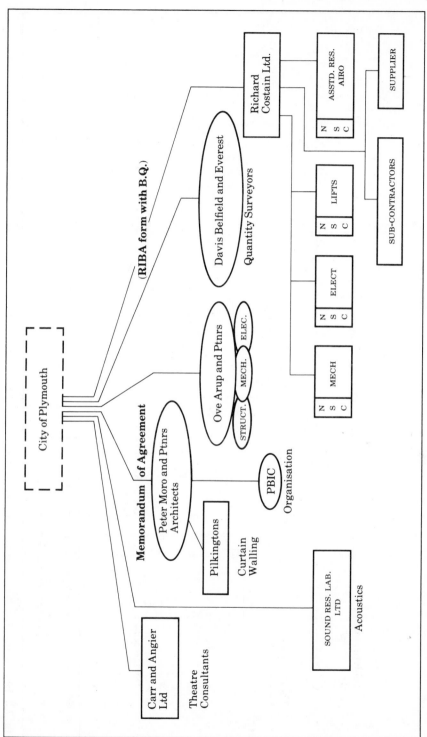

Fig. 7.3 (a) Plymouth Civil Theatre – Nexus of Contracts.

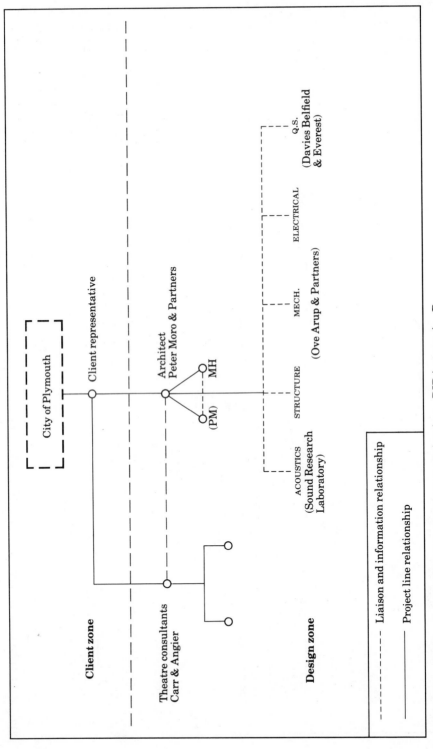

Fig. 7.3 (b) Plymouth Civic Theatre – project organisation – RIBA stage A – B.

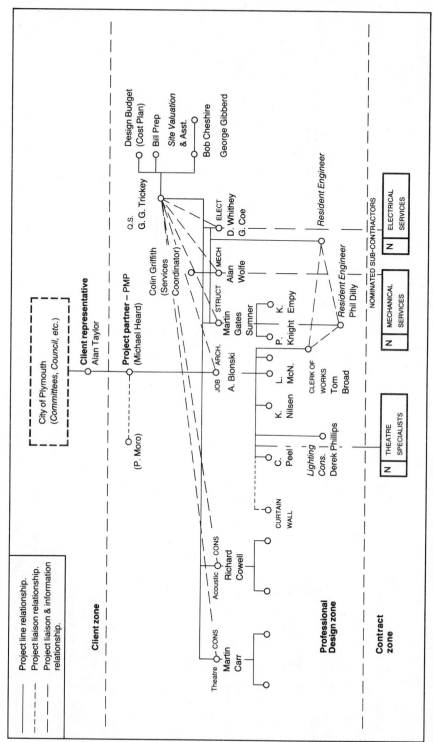

Fig. 7.3 (c) Plymouth Civic Theatre – project organisation – design team – RIBA stages C – G.

117

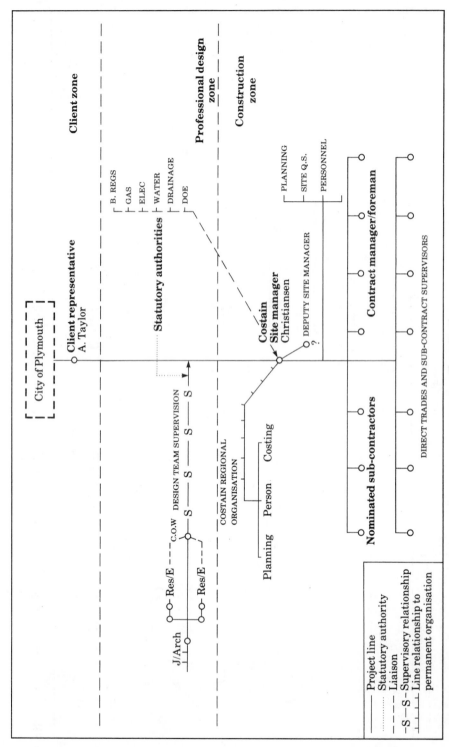

Fig. 7.3 (d) Plymouth Civic Theatre outline project organisation – construction team RIBA stage H.

This is like looking at each small part of a large map and therefore needing to identify the relationship of the job function defined against the person carrying it out and also how he relates to others in the organisational framework.

Many companies who are involved in continuing operations on a single large site, such as a motor car manufacturer, devote a great deal of effort to defining the roles and responsibilities of people who have worked and will work in that 'static' structure for many years. The effort is worth while because it eliminates waste by overlap or undetected defects by default of people, all performing in a complex team organisation.

How much more important it is to provide a clear definition on a project where the people are not used to working regularly with each other. Where the situation is a dynamic and constantly changing one and one where physical reference points and physical demarcation of divisions, departments and offices do not exist at the start but are set in a fourth dimension of time so that their responsibilities are of themselves transient. Within the time cycle of the design and construction of a large building project, taking perhaps 5 years, the responsibilities and relationships will change several times.

The scale and degree of responsibility as between one designer and another with whom his work is interrelated will also vary and the people who are discharging these various functions might themselves change over the period within the functional responsibility of the post.

Maintain the Manual

Having set up the Project Operations and Procedures Manual it is therefore important to ensure that it is maintained up to date and including the name of the person currently discharging the responsibility. This is best done by the reissue of a complete new sheet replacing the old to all those who hold the manual when updating is required.

Each sheet, as illustrated on the 'Paperwork and formal recording procedures' should show to whom it is distributed. Not every holder of a Manual will need every piece of information. But, everyone with any management responsibility for any part of the work should have a Manual which includes the overall framework and at least the information on those to whom he has a direct upwards, sideways and downwards relationship.

Figure 7.3(d), outlines project organisation during construction stage, and shows how the management emphasis in the project structure has moved in line with the contractual commitments and is now direct from the client representative to the site manager. The professional designers now have a liaison and supervisory relationship but no direct management authority.

119

The exercise of direct management authority by the design team would require in principle the approval of the client through the client representative and if given would then require a Variation Order varying the main contract. This concept may be difficult for both the 'amateur' client representative and the design team to grasp but it is the failure to observe these separate line relationships that is the biggest single cause of contractual disputes and also of claims against architects and engineers!

PETER MORO & PARTNERS	OPERATION & PROCEDURE MANUAL
PLYMOUTH CIVIC THEATRE	Ref: POP/
ORGANISATION STRUCTURE	Orig: July 1979
PROJECT ORGANISATION STRUCTURE & RELATIONSHIPS	Date Revised:

1. The successful completion of the project, particularly in terms of time and cost, will depend upon the effectiveness of the organisation brought into being to coordinate and control the efforts of the whole Design and Build Team. Some of those involved will have no other work commitments during the operation, others will have several. All will have, however, permanent commitments and responsibilities to their 'parent' organisation and conflicts of responsibility or objective are therefore possible.

2. These project procedures are intended to define the management objectives, roles, responsibilities and relationships of all those involved in the project and so clarify communications and authorities for all involved.
   They are intended to clarify and not conflict with the contractual obligations entered into between the parties.

3. The assumption behind each 'job mandate' is that the person appointed to the task accepts the role, responsibilities and relationships shown in this organisational procedure, and has had the approval/confirmation of his 'parent' organisation to the mandate.

4. It is accepted that the individuals fulfilling some of the roles may change; for this reason names are given in (parenthesis). Changes in post, which should be notified in advance to the Job Architect, will not therefore alter the mandate. Where the incumbent of the post on the project structure draws his authority essentially from his own organisation it will be generally appreciated if any changes intended by that organisation are discussed, prior to their becoming effective, with the Architect's Project Partner and Job Architect.

5. On receipt of this Procedure Note everyone named should therefore consider the implications and if anything is either unclear or apparently unacceptable for some reason related to contractual or other obligations which are not known to the Architects, a draft of the amendment desired should be sent to the Job Architect within 7 days.

6. The effectiveness of the operation will result partly from efforts of the individuals involved, partly from the mechanism of their formal relationship and partly from the paperwork flow instructing and recording their activities. The procedures by which the project will be controlled are therefore grouped into:-
   A. The purpose, function and authority of the various individuals involved – Project Mandates
   B. The purpose, function and authority of meetings held – Meeting Mandates
   C. The paperwork flow and formal recording procedures.

Fig. 7.4 Project mandates

PETER MORO & PARTNERS	OPERATION & PROCEDURE MANUAL

PLYMOUTH CIVIC THEATRE
ORGANISATION STRUCTURE
PROJECT MANDATES – MEETINGS

Ref: POP/
Orig: July 1979
Date Revised:

---

1. During the progress of the work on site (through RIBA Plan of Work Stages H, I, J, K, L) progress and coordination will be assisted by the holding of formal meetings of different groups involved in the operations. These are:-
   - Architect's Site Meeting
   - Q.S. Site Meeting
   - Contractor's Site Meeting
   - Design Team Meeting

   Their purpose, status and functions are as follows.

2. Architect's Site Meeting
   i) Purpose – To review progress and so consider in advance problems likely to arise in the future which can be resolved by the presence of the responsible designers and the contractor.
   ii) Status –
      a) This is the principal meeting to effect coordination and implementation of the Design by the Contractor's Building Team. It will be held regularly, normally at monthly intervals, and at such other times as considered necessary by the Job Architect.
      b) It will be attended by every project engineer/consultant and by the Contract Valuation Surveyor, or by their representative who should normally be authorised to discharge the engineer's responsibilities, and by the Contractor's Site Manager and approved support staff, and at appropriate stages by the sub-contract managers for each nominated sub-contractor.
      c) The Job Architect will take the chair.
      d) The Client Representative, Architect's Project Partner, and a senior representative of consulting firms may attend in an ex-officio capacity.
      e) The Project Architect may invite (from time to time) other representatives from firms involved as he considers desirable.
   iii) Minutes will be taken and issued to all attending by the Architects.

3. Quantity Surveyor's Site Meeting
   i) Purpose – The Contract Valuation Surveyor will visit the site from time to time to carry out his duties. To assist him he may call either regularly or as he considers necessary a Site Meeting of the Contractor's Quantity Surveyors and those appointed by any nominated sub-contractor.
   ii) Status –
      a) These meetings will be concerned only with the valuation of the works and will be the sole concern of the Contract Valuation Surveyor.
      b) They will not normally be attended by other members of the Design Team, and will have no formal status under the building contract(s).
      c) The Valuation Surveyor may issue minutes should he choose to do so, in which case a copy will always be sent to the Job Architect.

4. Contractor's Site Meeting
   i) Purpose – The Site Manager will hold regular site meetings of his site team, nominated and other sub-contractors to effect coordination of the Construction Team.
   ii) Status – The meeting will be concerned only with matters of management which are the General Contractor's sole contractual responsibility. Any minutes that are taken will not be circulated to the Design Team.
      The General Contractor will decide who should attend and the Job Architect

.... Project mandates

or his representative, the Design Engineering Consultants or their representatives, the Quantity Surveyor's Contract Valuation Surveyor or his representative, will attend only at the express invitation of the Contractor's Site Manager.

5. Design Team Meeting
   During the progress of works on site, particularly in the early period, there will be an overlap with the completion of the design. Meetings of the Design Team which have taken place throughout Phases D – G may therefore continue.
   i) Purpose – The purpose of these meetings, as was the case during the design phases, is to ensure continued coordination of the design process.
   ii) Status – The meeting will be attended by the nominated representative of each of the Design Consultants and the Quantity Surveyors, by the Job Architect, (who may deputise for the Project Partner in taking the Chair), and by the Architect's Team Leader, who may be accompanied by members of their respective design teams.
       Decisions taken, particularly as to functional needs, time and cost, will be minuted and circulated to all of the Design Team.
   At later stages in the construction of the works meetings of the Design Team may well be held separately from the Architect's Site Meetings to clarify points of design or prepare design modifications within the existing scope of the contract, or to deal with Variations. The Job Architect will normally take the Chair on these occasions.

6. Ad Hoc Meetings
   Additional 'Design Team' Meetings between two or more, but not all members of the Design Team, may be held to consider specific problems that may not affect all. These will follow a similar format, be numbered in sequence and minutes will be issued to ALL who receive Design Team Meeting Minutes.

PETER MORO & PARTNERS	OPERATION & PROCEDURE MANUAL	
PLYMOUTH CIVIC THEATRE ORGANISATION STRUCTURE	Ref:	POP/
	Orig:	July 1979
PROJECT MANDATE – CLIENT REPRESENTATIVE	Date Revised:	

1. The Client shall appoint a Client Representative to act as the focal point for all communications between Client and Design Team on the one hand and the Construction Contract Team on the other.

2. All contractual matters shall be submitted by the Project Partner to the Client Representative and his authority will be sought on any matter connected with a variation to:-
   i) the Client's Brief;
   ii) the authorised design, or
   iii) amendments required as a result of constructional necessity or to the authorised programme for completion.

3. The Client's Representative may be invited to attend Architect's Site Meetings. He will receive copies of the minutes of the Architect's Site Meetings, Architects Instructions, Contractor's Quarterly Report and advice of contract variations.

4. He will be responsible for ensuring that payments are made by the Client to the General Contractor, to the Architects and to other members of the Design Team in accordance with their contracts with the Building Owner.

.... Project mandates

PETER MORO & PARTNERS	OPERATION & PROCEDURE MANUAL	
PLYMOUTH CIVIC THEATRE PROJECT	Ref:	II/MR
MANAGEMENT RESPONSIBILITIES	Orig:	July 1979
PROJECT PARTNER – MICHAEL HEARD	Date Revised:	July 1979

Accountable to the Partnership for:-
  i) The fulfillment of the Client's brief in respect of design and specification to meet the functional, aesthetic and cost requirements;
  ii) Preparing project budget and obtaining Partners' approval to resources required;
  iii) Direct client relationship with functional responsibility to client representative for all matters of contractual relationships in respect of PM&P and all design consultants, quantity surveyors and main building contractor;
  iv) Establishing the design team and chairing meetings of the design team;
  v) Establishing office design budget and programme and agreeing this with subordinates and associated design consultants. Controlling project costs;
  vi) Establishing project structure and delegating authority for each stage and area of activity, particularly with regard to Job Architect;
  vii) Obtaining guidance from other partners as required.
  viii) Ensuring that fees are issued to Clients when due.

PETER MORO & PARTNERS	OPERATION & PROCEDURE MANUAL	
PLYMOUTH CIVIC THEATRE PROJECT	Ref:	II/MR
MANAGEMENT RESPONSIBILITIES	Orig:	July 1979
JOB ARCHITECT – ANDRZEJ BLONSKI (during RIBA Activity Phases E to M)	Date Revised:	July 1979

Responsible to – Project Partner – Michael Heard.
Accountable for –
  i) Detail design (within undefined limits)
  ii) Implementation of the Project in accordance with the drawings, specification to achieve completion 25th September 1981. Time and cost programme. Supervising the works on site in accordance with the main and any sub-contracts.

In particular he will:-
  iii) Chair all Architects' site meetings;
  iv) Issue all Architect's Instructions and authorise directions given by the Clerk of Works;
  v) Authorise and issue all orders deviating the contract when Project Architect has received client approval.
  vi) Sign all certificates and issuing fee account.

In the event that further drawings or design work is needed he will:-
  vii) Ensure that this is carried out to meet the requirements of the Contractor's agreed programme, seeking advice or assistance as he considers necessary from the Project Partner, and:
  viii) If additional resources over the agreed programme are required obtain the Project Partner's approval to the use of these additional resources.

Accountable to the Job Architect are:-
  i) The Clerk of Works in accordance with his Job Specification;
  ii) Those Architects and Assistants allocated to the project team
  iii) The design consultant's representatives shown on the organisation diagram.

PETER MORO & PARTNERS	OPERATION & PROCEDURE MANUAL
PLYMOUTH CIVIC THEATRE ORGANISATION STRUCTURE	Ref: POP/
	Orig: July 1979
PROJECT MANDATE – STRUCTURAL ENGINEERING DESIGNER Ove Arup & Partners (Peter Knight)	Date Revised:

1. The Project Structural Engineer nominated by Ove Arup & Partners to the project team shall be accountable to the Job Architect for the design of all structural engineering work within the agreed cost limits for the work and for preparing a programme for the execution of this work.

2. Once agreed, he shall be responsible for ensuring that the work is produced in accordance with the time programme, or for notifying the Job Architect when delays are likely to occur as a result of the failure of others in the Design Team to provide information in time for the Engineer to maintain his programme.

3. He will attend all Design Team Meetings.

4. He will advise the Job Architect on the implications of any instructions given by the Resident Engineer on his behalf on site (which will have been authorised) by the Architect's Clerk of Works – See Clerk of Works' Mandate) before the Architect issues Confirmatory Instructions.

5. He will coordinate the work of any Structural design assistants who may assist him in relation to the project and the Resident Engineer on site (Phil Dilly) will be accountable to him for the discharging of his duties.

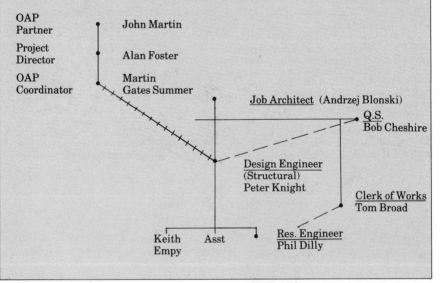

.... Project mandates

PETER MORO & PARTNERS   OPERATION & PROCEDURE MANUAL

PLYMOUTH CIVIC THEATRE   Ref: POP/
PROJECT ORGANISATION
                       Orig: July 1979
PAPERWORK & FORMAL RECORDING Date Revised:
PROCEDURES

In addition to the Conditions of Engagement which define contractual obligations of
the design team to the client and the general contract on the RIBA Form which is the
basis of the contract between the Contractor and the Client, the project will be
administered and recorded by minutes and paperwork control systems as follows:-

   i) Minutes of Design Team Meetings.
  ii) Minutes of Architect's Site Meetings.
both of which will note all items discussed and record formal decisions taken at the
meetings.
 iii) The Clerk of Works will issue Directions on the standard RIBA Form
      (attachment A), which will also incorporate Directions initiated by Resident
      Engineers for the Design Consultants which are authorised by him.
  iv) The Clerk of Works Weekly Report Form (attachment B).
   v) Architect's Instructions issued on the RIBA form, which will verify Clerk of
      Work's Directions and also indicate the authority or cause in order to assist with
      the determination of items which will constitute a justifiable Variation to the
      contract in either time or cost.
  vi) Advice of Contract Variation, ACV, which will be issued by the Architect to
      inform the client of agreed contractual variations (this assumes that the client's
      authority will have been obtained earlier to the Variation if it is not the result of
      an essential requirement for constructional reasons).
 vii) The Contractor's Quarterly Report, which will be issued direct by the Contractor
      to the Client, with a copy to the Architect.

The distribution of all paperwork should be shown on the document itself as indicated
on this Procedure Note. The coding for distributions are:-

F   –   Full distribution;
ADT   –   All Design Team;
ASM   –   All attending Architect's Site Meeting;
CR, Th, Ac, S,   Particular adressee only, or additional to other circulation, e.g.: ADT
M, E, Arch, QS,   + COW = All Design Team plus Clerk of Works; or ADT − CR = All
COW   Design Team less Client Representative.

Fig. 7.4   Project mandates − Extracts from Project Operation Manual.

Case Study 3 illustrated dramatically what can happen when these
principles are ignored. At this stage, with an efficient contractor and a
good site organisation, it may be sensible to delegate the task of
maintaining the Project Manual to the contractor, and probably to the
site manager (who had a deputy for whom this could have been a
sensible 'operating management' task). In this particular case of the
civic theatre, the responsibility was maintained by the architect's project partner who had instigated the procedures and kept in close touch
with the whole project throughout the construction period, and was
effectively the 'job architect' throughout RIBA Stage 'H'.

The existence of a Project Operations and Procedures Manual and its maintenance by the project manager certainly poses an additional task and imposes a further framework of documentation upon the project. But it will go a long way to prevent disputes and differences from arising and will certainly generate far less paper than that produced by any contemporary construction dispute at present in litigation or formal arbitration – and it will all be pre-classified and indexed!

Good project organisation and paperwork are certainly an essential element in dispute prevention for all firms engaged in construction, design, contracting and subcontracting. Many contractors will say that with the degree of competition now existing this is not possible – or indeed that as far as they can, they do this already – but that pricing the work depends much more on the visible extent of the preparation of the detail design so that the contractor can actually plan his work at the time of tendering and so price his intended operations rather than the measured quantities and labours set out in the bill.

Certainly, I know that for some time some contractors have priced up a job separately using their estimators, and where the construction details permit also using their planners to arrive at a total planned cost.

I know of one international contractor who told me that it took a great deal of courage to submit his bid for the first time on the basis of his planner's lower estimate, but to my first-hand knowledge it resulted in an acceptable tender. Despite some apprehension by the client (because the bid was lower than the general run of the others) the work went ahead and came out in accordance with the planner's estimate, and 2 weeks ahead of the scheduled contract period.

There were some minor modifications to details but by good management of the client and the design team, these were made sufficiently far in advance so that good communications produced a really integrated total activity and enabled all involved to fulfil their objectives.

C. Construction stage project management

Contractors can help support good management by the design team but the effects of this approach may be long term. In the shorter term, and perhaps on every project where one does not already exist, the contractor can initiate a Project Mandate and Procedures Manual.

In this he can establish the relationships and responsibilities for his own personnel, and for all the subcontractors. He can then ask the design team and the client to add those within their areas of activity. This will at the least alert both the professional groups and the client to the importance the contractor puts on good management, project structure and good communications.

The contractor's contribution to improved communications

In Chapter 4, I suggested that management must be practised in four directions, but for the contractor involved on large or international contracts his capacity to manage in at least three of the four directions is severely constrained in management terms by:

(a) the client and professionals;
(b) subcontractors;
(c) other contractors and authorities with operational responsibility for the site, project or works.

These, coupled with the unknown nature of the sub-ground works and weather, provide, as we have seen, a built-in recipe for conflict.

Twentieth-century technology has demanded new organisation structures and patterns – package deals, joint ventures, fast tracking, management contracting, design and build, entrepreneurial and other systems. All have their own standards and special contractual forms and can be even bigger recipes for disaster for contractors and clients alike.

What then can the contractor's project management do to minimise their effect?

Essentially, since we are concerned with those matters that cause contractual dispute rather than with the contractor's own internal management, this means what can the contractor do to influence the client and design team's management practices? Many of these will, and should, have already been in use for some time before the contractor arrives on the scene.

The first option open to the contractor in an attempt to be master of his own destiny must be to be selective in the projects for which he is prepared to tender, and then to price into his tender a minus factor where he knows that the design team is and has been well managed; and conversely, where it has not, to add accordingly for the possibility of an interference (there is another word for it on most sites!) factor that will limit the contractor's own freedom and ability to manage once his tender has been accepted.

If the client and design team comply then the desired position will have been achieved, and a spirit of co-operation and goodwill established, an excellent situation at the commencement of the project, and one which mirrors the approach to good management in large corporations where good management ideas are encouraged, in the McGregor vein, to flow 'upwards'.

If not, then the contractor will have established evidence of his attempts to create a good environment for the successful administration of the job, if a dispute should subsequently develop.

A further proposal which the contractor could always put forward, if it has not already been included in the contract documentation, is that a **Contract Management Adjudicator** should be appointed.

If the employer is a member of the BPF it is likely that such an allowance has already been made or an appointment is open for consideration.

In any event, the contractor who puts this suggestion forward immediately the contract has been signed will hardly be viewed in a worse light than one who instructs his claims department to bring forward all those areas that were spotted when the tender was prepared as the way to boost his return once the contract had been signed!

I know at least one architect of national repute who used to instruct the staff to ring all contractors who had been asked to tender for one of his jobs and ask to be put through to the contractor's 'claims department'. If they were – thus acknowledging the existence of the department – they were immediately taken off the tender list! But that was a few years ago. Now he accepts the situation as a 'normal' one forced upon contractors, although whether the result of fierce competition or poor management by the design team, or both, few would be prepared to say.

The appointment of an Adjudicator is both a means of prevention and an alternative means of resolution, and as it is a relatively new concept the procedure and its implications are dealt with in depth in Chapter 8.

Quality assurance management procedures

Much of the foregoing has been practised by many of the better firms in the construction industry, and for some years. But, because projects are multi-faceted and many firms are involved, not all of whom have, or practise, effective management, conflicts still develop. Building owners who are themselves sometimes partly the cause of the problem nevertheless feel forced to take action against the contractor or members of the design team, when the standard of performance they expected does not materialise from their project.

In 1983 the Government, through the Department of Trade & Industry, launched its National Quality Campaign for manufacturing firms. At the time of writing this has begun to extend its effect into the construction industry, and also to its professional design firms, who are seeking to ensure that their organisation conforms to British Standard 5750 for Quality Systems.

This identifies the basic discipline and specifies the procedures and criteria to ensure the service meets the customer's requirements.

BS.4778 Defines 'Quality' as 'The totality of features and characteristics of a product or service that bears on its ability to satisfy a given need.' Simply 'fitness for purpose'.

In the context of building fitness for purpose has been explored as satisfying the functional, aesthetic, cost and time requirements of the building owner.

What has not been done is to attempt to quantify the cost of what BS.6143 defines as 'Quality Related Costs – the expenditure incurred in defect prevention and appraisal activities and the losses due to external and internal failure'.

These include:

1. Defect prevention costs (quality management system, investigating, preventing and reducing defects)
2. Appraisal costs
3. Internal failure costs (discovered before handover)
4. External failure costs (discovered after handover)

Management information systems to provide Quality Related Costs (Q.R.C.) in the design and construction process need to incorporate both corporate (i.e. within an individual firm) and project Q.R.C. In the construction industry Q.R. Costs include the frequent and often enormous costs of dispute whether resolved by arbitration, litigation, or claim-handling procedures. All of these arise out of poor quality control, not necessarily within an individual corporate firm but arising from the ineffective interfaces between design and construction which (according to BRE studies) account for 90% of building failures. They also produce many of the dispute situations.

The five keys to success in quality assurance are:

1. Good communications
2. Good information systems
3. Good participation
4. Good monitoring of system in use
5. Good training

of which 1, 2 and 4 must relate particularly to the project. The essence of the quality-assurance campaign is to have third-party certification by an accredited independent body that the system exists within a firm and is practised, which is done by means of an annual quality audit. If only firms who have been certified are used on projects this will go a long way to achieve the desired objective, but for the construction industry this is really only meaningful if the third-party certification related to the finished building — and over its prescribed (if it was) life span.

But, third-party certification of firms will go a long way to preventing many contractual disputes.

Adjudication over those disputes that remain as conflicts of interest develop between the parties involved in a project will further reduce quality related costs.

Contract Management Adjudication is in effect third party certification of project quality. When used the Adjudicator will have considered any claim made by either party that in effect the contract standards have not been met, and by his Award the Adjudicator will have indicated that the Project Quality Assurance standards have or have not been met.

If a project quality system has been used, and checked by the Adjudicator as a third party and no claims are made by any of the parties involved against another, there will be an even stronger indication that the project was properly considered and managed by all involved.

If for any reason complaints or litigation develops later, the project quality system will provide the best possible contemporary evidence that the defect was **not** the result of negligence!

CHAPTER 8

DISPUTE PREVENTION BY CONTRACT MANAGEMENT ADJUDICATION

Prevention is better than cure, and as has previously been said 'Good management is the preventive medicine of dispute.'

How then can better management be applied to situations of potential conflict between parties when situations arise unexpectedly which give rise to differences or disputes, particularly in one-off contracts?

Proverbially a stitch in time saves nine, and clearly the earlier a problem can be resolved the less chance there is for the dispute to escalate.

The principles of third-party intervention used early and dynamically to help the parties to resolve their problems will help to create a constructive atmosphere.

This process must not remove the authority or functions of those made responsible for the management of the project by their principals.

Rather, it should support the project's management procedures and give rulings or make Awards only when those in day-to-day control are unable to agree.

In the past, construction contracts have used the concept of third-party intervention in relation to resolving disputes at the end of the contract. Now the principle has been brought forward into the operations of the project where it can be of productive use by the BPF's system of project procedure and it has been incorporated in the 'Association of Consulting Architects 1984 Form of Building Agreement'. Polycon Consultants have also established techniques of dispute adjudication which provide practical methods for similar applications, all are compared and related to conventional arbitration.

Good management is an essential requirement for the satisfactory provision of the client's needs in all building projects, the complexity of which have grown out of all recognition of the nature of the Industry when first the architect was named in the RIBA form of contract and his responsibilities defined for the supervision of the works – and the contract.

As we have seen, Construction, with its plethora of parties, purposes and relationships, has a built-in climate for conflict. The design team which was charged first with the responsibility for establishing the client's needs in an interactive process to 'get the brief', must next create the design and decide upon the specification to fulfil these needs. It is axiomatic, therefore, that when the various contractors implement these designs any errors or ambiguities they find must reflect upon the work of the design team who, in today's more commercial and demanding situation, cannot sit as judge in their own cause. In any conflict the two parties to the contract – which is no more, but no less, than a complex set of legal promises from one to the other by the employer and the contractor – will inevitably be at odds with each other and either or both may equally be unsure of the actions or intentions of the third group – the designers – and so seek to blame them for the situation.

It is into this situation that arbitration or adjudication – the power to settle by a third non-involved party – is needed.

Indeed, the better and stronger the project management for one or the other party to the contract the more important will be the capacity to hold the balance fairly between them.

In full-scale arbitration under the 1950 and 1979 Acts and under the various forms of contract prior to the BPF's new system, the powers given to the Arbitrator 'to settle all matters in dispute between the parties' were almost sovereign and certainly greater than those possessed by a High Court judge or the Official Referee, but these powers come much too late, frequently many years and volumes of documentation after the event when one party or both have suffered the financial or practical disadvantages resulting from the dispute.

What is needed is to provide some of those powers to a third party to make a ruling as soon as is possible after the situation causing the dispute has arisen.

This is the role of contract management adjudication, an essential corollary to a strong project manager.

What form should this adjudication take? How should it be structured, and what powers should the Adjudicator have? And will it not usurp the authority and status of the architect or the engineer?

We have examined the way arbitration procedures developed outside of Construction to reflect the needs of practical business in Shipping and in the 'pinch and sniff' Commodity areas where the merchants who have bought and sold unseen but against a specified quality involve the arbitration of one of their fellow merchants. This merchant's skill is not necessarily greater than their own, but he has the essential status of not having been involved in that particular contract.

The benefits of arbitration under the 1979 Act now enable the parties to get a final and binding Award virtually free of the risk of appeal (subject only to technical misconduct by the Arbitrator) and so eliminate the costs that could flow from an appeal to a High Court judge or from the court of first instance to the Court of Appeal and thence to the House of Lords, and possibly even to the European Supreme Court.

Traditionally, arbitration arising from UK contracts has awaited the conclusion of the contract before an Arbitrator makes a final settlement of all matters in dispute. Today, the effect of inflation on major projects and the tensions that can develop as financial stringency and uncertainty arise from unresolved differences cannot await long-delayed settlements months or years after the event. Particularly so when construction disputes are queueing up for counsel's time and the costs and complexities of arbitration are beginning to approach, or even outstrip, those of the High Court.

How then to improve the position further? Quite simply, the answer is a quicker response to dispute resolution, more akin to that of the referee, umpire and line judges in sport whose instant decision is required to keep the balance between the highly paid combatants who grace the turf at Wimbledon, Lords or Wembley. In the case of the Construction Industry it is essential too that the judges have real knowledge and background experience as well as of the foundation of the dispute on a particular project.

However, most standard forms of contract used in construction projects contain Arbitration Clauses but sometimes one party involved in such a contract will be resistant to invoking the Arbitration Clause and using the benefits of Arbitration. Yet he will sometimes pursue his claim by 'negotiation' or arguing his case for anything up to 5 years or more after the completion of the project.

Many reasons are given for not using the procedure. That it is preferable to negotiate and so keep options open because this will be quicker. There is fear, and there is current evidence to support this fear, that the procedure will be expensive, time consuming and will be as bad or even worse than pursuing the matter through the Courts. There is ignorance and therefore fear of the procedure. There is a reluctance to lose the legal option. There is a fear that the parties will not be able to agree upon an Arbitrator – and so they are not prepared to accept in advance the finality of an Award from an unknown Arbitrator if the appointment is made by the President of some particular professional institution, and so on.

One of the benefits of Arbitration under UK law, and most other legal systems, is the finality of the Award. It is probably this very finality coupled with the unknown Arbitrator that leads to the rejection of third-party procedure.

But experience in both the USA and the UK, at least where technical matters are materially involved, has shown that if parties were to have the Award before them, before they are required to undertake their acceptance of it they will generally do so rather than face the costs, delay and harrassment that a civil action in the Courts would involve. Adjudication as a management technique to resolve technical disputes has been developed to have regard to all these natural resistances and to provide practical ways of overcoming them and so provide the best of both worlds.

Adjudication requires the parties to agree at the time of making the appointment of an Adjudicator:

1. that the Adjudicator should make an Award covering all matters in dispute;
2. the Adjudicator shall decide also who should pay the fees and costs involved in the Adjudication;
3. how long the parties shall have to accept the Award or to notify their rejection of it (with their reasons) after its issue;
4. that in the event that both parties do not accept the Award, the Adjudication findings and the Award may be used by either of them as evidence in any further Arbitration or Legal proceedings.

Figure 8.1 illustrates the procedures developed by Polycon Endispute Management Services to provide this Contract Adjudication procedure. It assumes that a difference already exists and that one party is, as is usually the case, more anxious to have it speedily determined than the other.

The technique Contract Adjudication implies that there is a contract between the parties, and accepts that this contract may include an Arbitration Clause, but the technique is applicable to any situation of dispute as long as there is some form of contract between the parties in dispute. If there is not, then an alternative technique known as Dispute Adjudication exists.

Contract Adjudication was intended for use after the completion of a project but can also be applied when works are still in progress. The Adjudicator's terms of reference might then be extended to cover the monitoring of the works that continue contemporaneously with, or after the Adjudication Award has been published and accepted.

The Adjudicator does not either usurp the authority of those whose job it is to manage or supervise the continuation of any works. But he would be available to adjudicate on any matter where the parties, or their agents, such as engineer, surveyor or architect, were unable to agree with the other side on the basis of continued progress.

Modifications to the technique of third-party Adjudication and Award to provide preventive measures for dispute are incorporated in the further development of the technique by Polycon, which make it suitable for use from the time the contract for a large project is signed. This

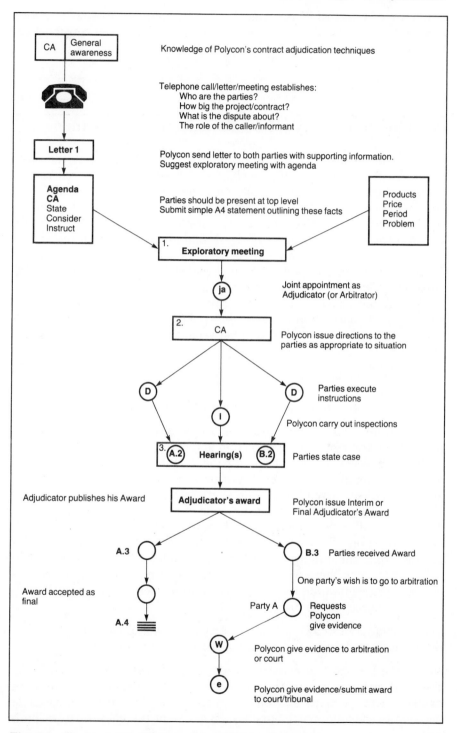

Fig. 8.1 Contract adjudication after difference has arisen.

is known as Contract Management Adjudication, which is seen as the essential corrollary of good project management on large construction projects.

Adjudication – a dynamic management procedure

It was against the background of client dissatisfaction that the BPF developed their system with the objective of, as they saw it, redressing the balance more in favour of the building owner who, after all, they say, is the customer of all the various parts of the Construction Industry. The BPF system recognises for the first time the conflicts of interest between the various members of the design and construction team; and the problem of asking the architect or engineer to be judge-in-his-own-cause whilst maintaining a continuing contractual relationship with the employer. The BPF system embraces many management maxims that have been developed by the better firms within the conventional framework of the Construction Industry, but the one really new concept – the essential one in terms of balance between conflicts of interest – is the appointment of *Adjudicators*:

(a) **as between the client and the design team** – in Stages 1–4 of the system; and
(b) **between the client and the contractor** – in Stage 5 of the system.

It was quite separately, a group of experienced professionals, senior members of their several construction and management professions, and including several very experienced panel members and a past President of the Chartered Institute of Arbitrators, who made their study over several years of current needs and past practices in dispute resolution.

This recognised the need for a means of resolving problems **during**, rather than after the completion, of long-term and complex projects such as construction. They recognised too that whilst there are benefits arising from the finality of Arbitration under the 1950 (and 1979) Arbitration Acts there were many companies who would not make use of these procedures for reasons which were principally concerned with having to agree to this finality:

(a) in advance of knowing who the Arbitrator would be; and
(b) what the extent of any Award 'against' them might be.

In a large hierarchical corporation the chief executive is used to being the final 'arbiter' within the corporation and the final 'negotiator' in external arrangements and was loath to give up this ultimate power of decision to some unknown outsider. So out went the baby with the bath water!

Yet, experience in both the USA and the UK when a different approach was tried resulted in those same executives first recognising and then accepting an Award arrived at by a process akin to arbitration but one which was much quicker, and more cost-effective. Providing they did not have to accept its ultimate finality in advance!

The objectives of the BPF and the Polycon approach to contract adjudication are identical and the methods used are very similar. The purpose of both approaches is to ensure the better management of complex construction projects. Both systems recognise, as an essential ingredient in the project's management, the need for an outside Adjudicator to resolve disputes during progress, but without necessarily prejudicing either party's ultimate legal rights at the end of the project.

Polycon's experience and approach reflect their arbitration and management consultancy experience across all areas of the Construction Industry. The differences of approach between Polycon's and the BPF adjudication are therefore only on the practical and procedural aspects.

Polycon recognises that in Construction, 'events', both foreseen and unforeseen, produce 'situations', but disputes arise between people. This is principally because there will always be differences and variations between offer and acceptance (and therefore tender and contract). But by reason of their differing backgrounds, experience and approach and because their objectives come into conflict, the people involved divide and disputes arise.

Initially the client, the client representative, the design team and the general contractor all have a common objective – the completion of the project at the right time and cost to satisfy the functional needs and aesthetic concepts. To achieve this it is right that the client's views and requirements are paramount throughout. This in its turn, as the BPF system recognises, necessitates effective management of the project, the allocation of responsibilities and the recognition of any overlaps in authority and definitions of accountability.

But nothing in even the most effective project management structure can deal with the fundamental principle that there will always be two parties who could come into conflict and thus require a third party, knowledgeable of the situation, to hold the balance of fairness when such disputes arise.

The BPF system recognises that adjudicators, available immediately when needed, have specific duties related to the contract and the parties. The system requires the adjudicators to have a wide range of skills, to have a neutral status in relation to all the parties involved and to exercise their skills *judicially* and in the interests of progress of the project. These resources, facilities and the integrity with which they are deployed must be regarded as an essential and as perhaps the most beneficial item *of* cost of the contract.

In both the preliminary stages and during construction the skills required must reflect, although not be a mirror image of, the skills and

Benefits of Arbitration		Benefits of Adjudication
Chief features worthy of trust		Cost benefits
• Privacy	— ✓	
• Certainty of application	— ✓	(Upon agreement)
• Equality of parties	— ✓	
• Competence of Arbitrator	— ✓	Multi-disciplinary • •
• Fast and inexpensive	— ✓	• •
• Legal effectiveness	— ✓	Subject to review after publication
• Certainty of enforcement	— ✓	ditto
		Plus
		• Over 50% saving in cost over litigation
		• Great savings in time
		• Reduction in stress for parties

Fig. 8.2 Benefits of arbitration and adjudication.

experience provided in the conception, design development and detailing of the project and its organisation, time and cost management. But the adjudicators should not be seen as 'over-managers' who will take over and usurp the authority provided to, by and for the various parties involved in the project.

The role of the Adjudicator is much more akin to the cricket umpire who will answer the question 'Howzat?' only when asked and whose other duties are strictly limited to monitoring performance in accordance with the rules.

Prompt, impartial adjudication is the essential corollary of strong project management.

Certain principles should therefore be established:

(a) For the Adjudicator to be, and remain available, he must have a commitment to, and therefore a contract with, both principal parties.

(b) Since the scope for potential adjudication is wide a 'team' of adjudicators should be available and be known to be accepted by the parties since it is this prior acceptance that provides the Adjudicator's authority.

(c) Disputes in Stage 5 will, or may, reflect back to decisions taken by the design team in Stages 3 and 4 which may have been the subject of an adjudication at that stage. It is therefore essential that there should be no discontinuity or inconsistency between adjudications in the overall framework of the project.

(d) The requirement for adjudication can best be provided by a single tribunal appointed to oversee the whole project.

(e) The tribunal must be multi-disciplinary, experienced, and have professional integrity in design, construction and the legal and contractual conditions.

(f) The Adjudicator's personal authority must be acceptable to both (all) parties.

(g) The appointment must be agreed between the parties and the appointment made as soon after the main contract is signed as possible.

Contract management adjudication

The role of this tribunal, essentially a dynamic one, will be contributing substantially to the management of the project and for this reason has been called contract management adjudication (CMA).

An Adjudication Tribunal jointly appointed by the parties to a contract as a separate contract will provide for the resolution of disputes as they arise at a relatively trivial cost. A cost probably far less than an insurance premium which, if as with all insurance premiums, the service is not required will have been the best provision to be made.

If the provision has to be used, the investment would have already paid off. Its cost would fall where the CMA Adjudicator objectively assessed which of the parties should meet the cost. Thus, all the other parties would immediately benefit from their investment foresight, and could proceed with their part of the project – productively.

When the building contract is signed, or shortly afterwards, the CMA team is appointed jointly by the parties to the contract and any subcontracts. The tribunal is retained for the period of the contract, to be available within 7 days of notice, on the request of any of the signatories, to decide any matter referred to it that is related to or arising from the contracts involved.

As part of the authority by their contract of appointment, members of the team would also be required to determine, like an Arbitrator, who should pay the costs of the reference and of the decision or Award. The parties may either accept the decision fully, and thus end that dispute, or notify that they may still wish to bring a claim at the end of the contract. In any event, until then they would be bound by contract to comply with the CMA decision.

In this the CMA differs from the BPF approach which proposes that the costs of the Adjudicator's fees is shared equally between the employer and the contractor. The BPF suggests that this will give the parties a mutual incentive to settle and not to prevaricate over the issues. The principle as developed by normal arbitration is that 'costs follow the event', i.e. the loser pays, which is a far greater deterrent to recalcitrant parties – and to those resisting legitimate and reasonable claims made in the daily progress of the project.

Further analysis of the CMA function identifies three distinct aspects of such a management procedure and therefore three distinct 'modes', each with its own functional purpose and separate implications:

1. **The initial appraisal** – on appointment, when the Adjudicator must make an examination of the project contract in sufficient depth only to be able to give specific directions to the parties on the rules that must be applied to invoke the adjudication services if needed;
2. **The monitor mode** – during which the Adjudicator is retained purely to hold himself ready to give a decision when asked; and
3. **The adjudication mode** – when the service is invoked and the Adjudicator exercises the authority given by the parties.

In the first phase – which corresponds to that of an Arbitrator satisfying himself that he has the competence and jurisdiction and over what submission – will necessarily involve in large contracts a perusal of all the contract documents – the memorandum of agreement, the contract drawings, specification, bill of quantities, contract organisation, programme, etc.

Experience has shown (for example in Case 3 in Ch. 7) that the seeds of many contractual disputes are already sown at the time the project commences and in the course of the initial appraisal the Adjudicator can render a highly valuable service to both parties by notifying any gaps or overlaps in the documents, the organisation, and perhaps in some cases even the technology.

Experience is that problems occur most frequently on long or complex projects if lines of communication and the lines of contract are not co-ordinated at the outset. The initial appraisal can show up if these need to be clarified or tightened up.

Having noted any areas of possible problems it is clearly better to tell both parties what has been noted. These 'observations' are **not** advisory in the sense that the Adjudicator recommends any action, they are merely matters to which he draws the parties' attention. For example, he might observe that no single person has been appointed to be 'the client representative', or that the contractor has not established a subcontract for some particular key aspect of the project; or that no 'programme' network or bar chart, etc. has been established which would appear to be relevant to obtaining further information from the client or design team on outstanding details in a tight schedule, for, say, stage completion; or that costs, or drawing numbers, etc. did not tie up with each other.

In none of these matters is the Adjudicator removing, nor indeed is he able to remove, the authority of the various individuals who have been, or should have been, appointed to carry out the various tasks. All of these are matters which have been recited in Arbitration Awards made as an Arbitrator's findings, which in turn affected his Award, but which, had they been made at the right time, could have prevented the dispute arising, if the parties' attention had been drawn to them. Frequently, such matters are easy for the outsider, in this case looking to establish the invocation procedure and preventing disputes, to spot, whereas they have been overlooked by the parties each rushing about their respective activities at the start of the operations.

These observations would also be quite similar to an *obiter dictum* made by a judge – which have no effect on his judgment on particular matters before him.

It has been suggested that such observations would not be welcomed by a contractor whose claims department has already noted some of them and stored them up for use on an appropriate 'rainy day' to his own advantage. But the contractor generally makes his money from first planning and then performing in accordance with, or better than his plan, rather than keeping a trump card up his sleeve in case he needs it! In such a case there would be every reason to submit his 'claim' in advance, i.e. immediately the observation had been made, and to ask the Adjudicator for a ruling or Award – if he could not get a satisfactory one from the client or design team.

The Adjudicator's observations are not accompanied by suggestions to overcome or put right the points noted, but if asked – by **both** parties, i.e. if the problem is submitted for the Adjudicator's **ruling**, not advice – the Adjudicator could study the problem and either give further more detailed observations for those charged with the responsibility to make the decisions or, if asked, make an Award which the parties are then bound to implement and uphold at least until the end of the project. Figure 8.3 illustrates the procedure and the subsequent modes, and clearly identifies the different status of the Adjudicator in each of the three modes.

For the adjudication mode the Adjudicator is remunerated by a time-based fee – borne pro rata by the party responsible for the problem irrespective of who actually invokes the 'Hearing' and Adjudicator's Award.

The other two modes – appraisal and monitoring – are potentially of equal benefit to the parties involved, and the appointment fee is shared equally between them, as is the purely nominal retainer on a quarterly or annual basis. The fee level will clearly depend on the size, duration and complexity of the project, but will necessarily involve some time being spent on the documentary scrutiny before the invocation rules are issued.

If the contract has already been signed before the Adjudicator's appointment is made it is clear that the appointment fee will be seen to fall equally on the parties making the appointment, but on a complex project the procedures would apply not only to the contract between the

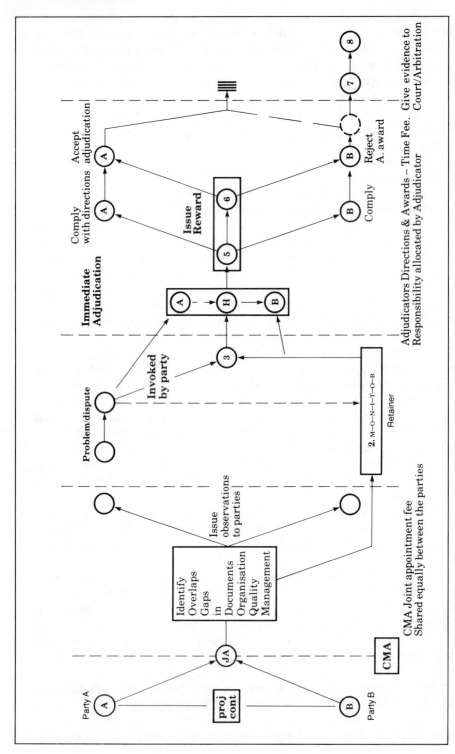

Fig. 8.3 Contract management adjudication during long term contracts – outline procedures.

employer and the contractor but also to the other contracts between the employer and the members of the design team, to any direct contracts, and nominated subcontracts between the employer and these other contractors. In principle this would also apply to contracts between the main contractor and his subcontractors. The fee would therefore be appropriately allocated.

If these conditions are written into the tender documents, as they should be, then contractors may well include their portion of the cost within the general provisions, but whether this would be as an addition to their general preliminaries pricing for overheads and profit, or as a reduction, only the estimator and director responsible for the tender would know!

The benefits of CMA procedures can be summed up as follows. They will:

1. Reduce avoidable delays during the progress of the contract;
2. Resolve dispute problems immediately a situation arises that might damage one of the parties or prevent them from proceeding with the work;
3. Reduce the costs to all parties involved in the dispute;
4. Eliminate the 'judge in own cause' and conflict of interest for the professionals whose earlier decisions are now at issue;
5. Record factually and objectively the situation as found so that expert, impartial, opinion will be available should any party wish to later join battle on the issue, or its consequences.

The full procedures of both the BPF adjudication system and Polycon's CMA are set out in Appendices I and II, but Fig. 8.5 compares each with conventional arbitration.

The matters raised and decisions called for will be essentially project management. They may affect the contractual, operational, financial or legal aspects of the project. For this reason the CMA appointment is a multiple appointment and a team might comprise architectural, surveying, engineering, legal, accountancy and personnel disciplines.

It is axiomatic that at the time of their being called in to determine matters, members of the team will hear all the representations and see all the evidence and will make appropriate documentary, photographic or other records. Thus, if any of the parties wish to take legal action later, their ultimate rights have not been surrendered. The CMA experts (whose services were *jointly* retained by equal payment from the parties) will be able to present the facts to any judge or formal Arbitration Tribunal to which recourse may be made after the end of the project, and so be truly impartial experts giving contemporaneous evidence.

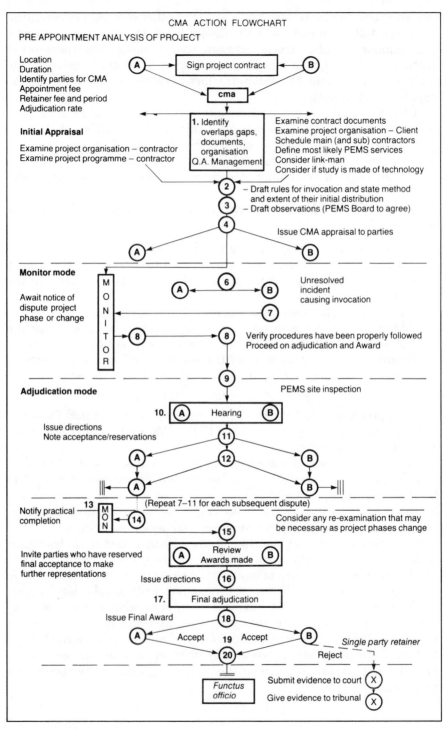

Fig. 8.4   Detailed CMA procedure flow diagram.

Corporate adjudication

In the case of Polycon's CMA technique, it is a company which is appointed Adjudicator and thus through the singular appointment all the professional skills and experience required of the tribunal are available under the corporate appointment.

This unique feature of the appointment merits further examination for it undoubtedly adds much to the practicality of appointing an Adjudicator at the start of multi-disciplinary long-term construction contracts, and it overcomes the practical disadvantages inherent in the BPF system (as shown by Fig. 8.5). There is a similar company which is operating in the USA and once the advantages are evident it would seem likely that there will be others established here.

The scale of large projects in Construction, and therefore of the organisations necessary to carry them out, grows even larger. Construction is not alone, indeed it is probably behind the trend over the last 50 years which has seen the number of motor car manufacturers reduce from nearly 200 to a mere handful in the UK whilst the design, development and production of a new aircraft requires the collaboration of the largest companies in three European countries to compete with Boeing, Lockheed and Douglas in North America.

This scale of operation demands vast resources and multi-disciplinary management teams to carry them out.

It is therefore essential that any adjudication over matters in dispute should reflect the range of technical expertise involved in the project and that the tribunal should itself be well managed.

Its resources and response must match the requirements of the technique, and be seen as part of a well-managed project operation. An *ad hoc* collection of individuals assembled as a result of an approach to an appointing president is hardly likely to be quickly effective and reliable, nor at a random point of time are the odds favourable that all the skills required will be possessed by those available – even if the match required between disciplines is appreciated by the appointing authority!

If speed and efficiency are required to improve performance on construction contracts and to prevent disputes developing the resources for the task must be readily available and developed to a suitable degree.

Final Adjudication Award

All CMA Awards made during the progress of the works are interim in that they are subject to final review and the making of a final Adjudication Award at the end of the project.

	BPF Adjudication system	Polycon Contract Management Adjudication	Conventional Arbitration
Objectives	1. Recognition of conflict of interest between: client and design team/ client and contractor	1. Better project management and control. Fewer disputes and quicker resolution of them before disputes exacerbate, to keep project moving but without sacrifice of ultimate rights by arbitration review after completion	Award of financial consequences of disputed action by technical expert with advice from legal assessor if necessary. Technical justice and equity with finality
	2. Recognition of conflict of interest between: client and design team/ client and contractor	2. Recognition of conflicting interest between: client and project management, client and design team, client and contractor/ subcont. and within any of the latter	
Timing of selection	A. Beginning of Stage 3 for design disputes	A. Whenever agreed – earliest is after appointment of client representative	After contract completed and formal notice of dispute served under the contract terms.
	B. Prior to invitations to tender for construction	B. Latest after dispute has arisen	Up to 5 years + after cause?
Timing of appointment	A. After dispute has arisen, nature of dispute identified, Adjudicator checked for suitability and availability and then again for acceptability to the parties – if available	A. Preferable – after Client Representative contract has been signed for Stages 1–4	After technical suitability has been verified and Arbitrator indicates he is prepared to act
	B. On dispute arising – again if still available and suitable for particular dispute	B. After construction contract signed for Stage 5	
	What if Adjudicator not prepared to act when dispute arises 'x' months after selection? Particularly if he has not been informed of his selection? Overbooking?		
Timing of adjudicators award	After investigation by Adjudicator minimum 5 weeks?	* Directions within 48 hours * Adjudication say 7 days * Final adjudication immediately following completion of contract	When both parties have completed their case preparation, etc. Say 9 months minimum after appointment?
Action on appointment	Will he (they) know of selection? Will he (they) be prepared to act? When,	1. On entering into Adjudicator's contract study nature, scope and	Issue directions for progress of dispute Hold preliminary meeting

	timing of client's contract(s). Look for overlaps and gaps in documents and organisation (? technology), make observations for benefit of both parties to **each** contract 2. Hold themselves in readiness for adjudication 3. Respond immediately to investigate issue directions and adjudicate (umpire) when invoked.		Final and binding subject only to misconduct and supervision by courts under 1950 and 1979 Arbitration Acts (if domestic)
Authority and award	where and how eventually required? Will he (they) have the right skills and time available without contract? All without financial commitment? Separate for Stages 2–4 for design team and from Stage 5 for construction. Both subject to review by Arbitrator after project completion	From client and from each party involved in project **after** each client contract (and subcontract) has been signed. Subject to review by Arbitrator only if parties give notice of non-acceptance after final adjudication after completion of project. If not – then Final and Binding	
Terms and conditions	Adjudication rulings must be complied with by parties until after project completion. Adjudicators' findings must be available as evidence before Arbitrator	All parties must comply with tribunal's rulings until after project completion. Adjudicators will decide on who should meet the cost of each adjudication. Adjudicators decide also how long parties shall have to reject final adjudication before it becomes final and binding under 1950/79 Acts	Give security for fees if required or pay fees before receiving Award after its publication. Others as agreed with Arbitrator or appointing body, or as defined in 1950 and 1979 Arbitration Acts
Fees	Time charges for Adjudicator payable equally by parties to adjudication. To be paid by clients within 14 days of rendering and half recoverable by him from other party	Appointment fee payable equally by parties to contract at time of appointment (lump sum 2–4 L/S for 5) Nominal retention fee payable by parties as agreed – based upon duration of contract, Stage 5. Reference and adjudication fee is time charge payable in accordance with Adjudicator's Award by parties responsible for action	Fees (and costs) normally follow event, i.e. shared or allocated by the Arbitrator according to cause

Fig. 8.5 Comparison chart – arbitration and adjudication techniques.

147

This final Award may be made either prior to the settlement of the final account or after its settlement – in which case it will take it into account in the final Adjudication Award.

The parties who appointed the Adjudicator have undertaken to abide by and comply with the Adjudicator's ruling throughout the period of the contract, and also to give notice within the prescribed period after each adjudication and at the end of the contract if they do not accept the Award as final.

Where more than one Award has been made, or where there is any matter which has not had final acceptance by both or all parties, the CMA Adjudicator will make a final Award and as part of that Award give a date by which it will be deemed to have become final and binding (and therefore, effectively, as if it were arbitration under the Acts) if no party gives written notice to the other, and to the Arbitrator, that he does **not** accept it and its finality. In this case he must also give with this notice his reasons for not accepting it.

The date will be fixed by the Adjudicator having regard to all the circumstances, but in a domestic construction dispute it will rarely be less than 21 days, nor more than 40, and generally just a little longer than the period used for the interim Award and notice, etc. which would have been set out in the directions at the time of appraisal.

On receipt of the final Award the parties will be in the position of knowing the cost (and benefit) to them and knowing that all the costs of that Award are behind them. They will also have a reasoned Award and the knowledge that 'their' experts have examined everything that they, their 'opponents' and the Adjudicators themselves have thought to be relevant, factually, technically and legally, and within the context, also of cost-benefit analysis. They will not have spent £500 to deliberate over whether £5 should go one way or the other depending upon which legal precedent was slightly more appealing. On the other hand, they will have given a thorough deliberation to all material matters, and the Award will have been scrutinised and countersigned by at least one other experienced Adjudicator who is a director of the company, thus ensuring that the Award is one which the company collectively and administratively is satisfied is proper in every respect.

This administrative review also investigates against a management and procedural checklist any apparent errors or shortcomings, and any minor differences that may seem to be present, so that these can be corrected – by the Adjudicator or Tribunal Chairman – before publication. A far more rigorous scrutiny than that given to any other Award – by Judge or Arbitrator!

Any party not satisfied can then assess what he might have to gain by rejecting the Award and going on, to what is virtually an appeal, either to arbitration or the courts. He can also expect that the costs he will incur will be far greater than those he has already met. He will also know that the Adjudicator will be available to give expert evidence to this further tribunal.

What a disputant may not realise is that with experts looking at many dispute situations they find that no matter who has appointed them they frequently agree on the technical facts – but only after they have both made their examination – and both written their reports and therefore incurred two (or more) sets of costs.

With the Adjudication Tribunal the parties only incur one set of costs – unless because of some inherent doubt he has, the expert feels he needs a second technical opinion and he feels justified in the interest of both parties (they are **both** 'his' clients) that his doubts if possible, should be removed by further technical debate.

Most experts are keen to get at the truth for themselves inquisitorially – the adversarial process of cross-examination to trip them up leads only to more careful expression and lack of firmness in their views rather than to the expression of a greater technical belief. But exercising the authority given to them and with immediate access to the facts, and to the views of the professional and technical people involved on the project should smooth the flow of the project. Under its original project managers satisfactory completion should be assured and with it the elimination of virtually all post-contractual dispute.

CHAPTER 9

PROFESSIONAL INDEMNITY INSURANCE AND DISPUTE PROCEDURES

The reasons for the high level of claims are examined and an analysis made of benefits that would accrue to the insured, the insured's client claiming damages for professional negligence and for the insurance underwriters from 'PICA' Professional Indemnity Contract Adjudication.

These are principally speed in settlement, much lower costs of processing, and a reduction of stress and expensive management time.

The methodology and operational procedures are set out, with two case studies quantifying the possible savings.

One area which in recent years has become increasingly prone to dispute is that concerned with the conduct of professionals *vis-à-vis* their clients. That is to say, the area for which architects, engineers, surveyors and others normally effect professional indemnity insurance.

This is partly the result of a generally more litigious climate, partly of the high incidence of building failures of relatively recent buildings, particularly those buildings where new techniques have been employed, and perhaps also of a change in the Insurance Industry's approach to this market for their services.

Many local authorities have decided that demolition is the best way to deal with the problems of high-rise flats where structural defects or maintenance problems are compounded by social dissatisfaction with the overall nature of the building. The original brief for buildings such as Ronan Point, now scientifically demolished, combined dramatic social change inspired by the client, who switched from small two-storey houses to tower-block flats, with financial stringency imposed by severe government cost yardsticks which posed the designers with particularly difficult new problems. This in turn prompted new solutions with new materials and techniques; but it has not deterred local authority clients from seeking redress for alleged negligence by both designers and constructors.

Local authorities and private organisations alike are suffering from the defects in flat roofs, from chemical interaction of new materials, from the failures of high alumina cement, and even new techniques with old and tried materials such as timber and tiles, but used in new ways.

Before they will appoint them, central and local government now require evidence of insurance from the professionals they commission for sums many times greater than their lifetime earnings. Yet, only a few years ago any architect who had effected professional indemnity insurance was, by the terms of the policy, forbidden to disclose its existence to anyone without the insurer's specific approval!

These problems have led to dramatically escalating premiums for building professionals generally, and for architects in particular, so much so that at the time of writing many architects have been unable to obtain effective insurance – at least at a cost which they can afford.

The Insurance industry generally has gone through several years where they have failed to recover the cost of their payments-out by their premiums and have therefore been forced to raise them considerably, but particularly in the area of professional indemnity insurance.

Assessing negligence

Excepting in the case of solicitors, any dispute over negligence of an insured professional is likely to be highly technical since it will always involve an assessment of a range of factors, but above all must answer the question: did the professional man exercise 'normal care and consideration', and did he show a normal standard of competence when judged against his peers, and the 'state of the art' at the time?

Negligence is not an absolute matter. Some professionals are generally expected to achieve success – and this would include architects, surveyors and engineers – as compared to doctors and lawyers involved in litigation who are not. 'Proof' will require 'expert' evidence – the opinion of another professional with knowledge of similar situations to assess the merits of every particular case brought by a client against his professional adviser.

The area is therefore one where the speedy and economic resolution of any dispute arising out of the use of the services of any professional is clearly in the interests of the professional, his client, and any other party whose actions are, or have been, involved in the subject area of the dispute.

Most, if not all, professional institutions maintain disciplinary procedures. These are designed to ensure and maintain standards of competence and integrity that the public at large should expect and should

151

obtain from members of their professional body. But the institutions can only deal with a general level of discipline and have no powers to extract damages for a client injured by a particular and specific negligence. That is why professional institutions in some cases recommend, and in others insist, that proper insurance cover is maintained by a practising professional to protect the interests of the injured client.

Latent risks

Another area of great importance to professionals involved in building design and construction are the risks they run for claims made against them many years after they have designed a project, when latent defects show up.

Building failures which occur perhaps 6 years after the building was completed, or 12 years after it was designed, and which cause damage not only to their client building owner but also to others using the building, has led to many cases against surveyors, architects or engineers being founded not on the professional's contractual relationships with his client but on a general tortious liability. The provisions of the Statute of Limitations give less protection to those involved in the design and construction of new buildings than they do in other situations.

The whole position of professionals and their indemnity insurance cannot be considered without having regard also to their liability for latent damage. The law relating to latent damage has recently been amended by Parliament but still can result in an architect finding that he is the subject of litigation long after he has retired from practice and is no longer covered by professional indemnity insurance. Even a designer's widow can find her husband's estate subject to attack from former clients claiming redress for latent damage!

Insurance companies and the professions are occupying their minds to find better ways of achieving the desirable result of protection for the client and protection for the professional – at a price that he can afford. Steps in this direction have been made in the development of new types of insurance such as the 10-year defects guarantee insurance which can be taken out by a building owner before the building is started. This can cover any latent defects which arise in the first 10 years of the building's life which is thought to be the period in which any defects that exist will show up. This will protect the client, the building owner, and ensure he has the funds immediately available to make good the damage, but the insurance company which underwrites the risk of a latent defect by project insurance will seek to recover its loss from those who are responsible for the loss, which could mean once again, the builder, the architect, the engineer or all of them in some proportion to be established.

Even if the insurance is taken out in the joint names of the building owner and all those involved in the operation and the insurance company waives its general right to subrogation the premium for waiving these rights will obviously be greater and it will still be necessary to establish the proportion of the premium to be paid by the building owner, the contractor, the architect and the engineer, etc.

Preventing dispute and reducing its cost

Indeed, unless there is some way of establishing responsibility between those who are involved, a general *laissez-faire* attitude between the various parties could develop which would only be tightened up by the additional scrutiny that the design receives from the project insurance underwriter's scrutineers, his professional watchdogs – probably engineers, surveyors and architects themselves – who will have to point out possible areas of error or negligence by the designers or they themselves could be subject to claims of negligence by their client, the insurers, and so on, in ever-increasing circles of claim, counterclaim, joinders and totally unproductive legal hassle.

In this situation the principles of adjudication discussed in Chapter 8 have a great deal to commend them.

Underwriting risk

Thus the role of professional indemnity insurance is to underwrite an architect or engineer's risks and indemnify him from acts for which he may become legally liable and for which damages may be awarded against him in a lawsuit or arbitration. It also indemnifies the insured for costs of the defence of any claim for legal liability. The majority of claims do not get to court and approximately 70 per cent of all monies paid out by underwriters are the costs of defending allegations rather than damages awarded against the insured. Adjudication procedures are designed to reduce this percentage, thus enabling lower premiums to be charged without detriment to the sums paid out in damages. Underwriters undertake to indemnify the architect or engineer from these damages. Frequently, therefore, it is also they who appoint solicitors to act in the defence of the action when an architect is at risk.

However, these solicitors are acting for their clients – the insurance underwriter. This may mean that they will act to protect the architect from claims made against him but it may also mean that they may be acting to protect **their** client, the underwriter, and not the architect. That he needs separate representation to protect his interests is often only appreciated too late by the architect or engineer under attack when he discovers that he is only partly covered or that the underwriters are prepared, in their own financial interests, to make a settlement with the claimant with which the insured professional does not agree.

Thus there is not only the potential for dispute between the professional and his client but also between the professional and his insuring underwriter.

If the insurance policy has been effected through an insurance broker the broker may help the professional to protect his position, but he too receives his commission from the underwriters and his position is therefore also a difficult one.

For both the insured and his insurers subject to a claim (and no less to the claimant) the redress of the financial imbalance from the failure of the original contract should be the main objective in the management of the dispute.

The present practice whereby 70 per cent of all payments-out made by underwriters goes on the process of settlement rather than in the settlement of the claim itself identifies the first and fundamental area for improved management performance. The 'contract adjudication' (see Fig. 8.1) technique should be able quite easily to reduce the fee costs by half – and sometimes far more – and so offer the opportunity for a substantial reduction in insurance premiums – and an increase in the profitability of the business to the insurers.

Reducing insured risk

Another technique, CMA (Fig. 8.4) – applied by the architect to his own contract with his client, and to his client's contracts with the contractors, etc. – will in the long term reduce both the risk of, and costs of, dispute in many of the areas at present the subject of claims. This will be particularly beneficial in project insurance for latent defects.

'Adjudication' is a dynamic management tool and should be used early and positively by parties in a variety of contractual and conflict situations. It is essentially third-party intervention by technically and legally qualified professionals 'jointly retained' by both parties to provide a multi-disciplinary judgment where conflicts of interest between the parties and their advisers exist.

Adjudication also seeks to provide cost-effectiveness by matching the cost of the resolution to the amount in dispute but at the same time without prejudicing any one party's freedom to proceed at his option.

The duty of care for an Adjudicator, as with an Arbitrator, is to both sides. But, it is reactive first to the technical facts and their commercial quantum, the arena in which the contract was most likely formulated. Probably it is also the arena which for most disputes in the architect's field will be one where justice will be more likely to be done and be seen to be done, than by transferring the dispute to the strictly adversarial system and procedures of the law and the courts.

The Adjudicator's role is as manager of a dispute situation, holding the balance between the sometimes conflicting extremes of custom and practices on the one hand, and law on the other, with sound commercial sense as a further, and in the indemnity insurance context, **the** most important criterion for both the professional and his insurer.

The relationship of broker to architect and underwriter and the purpose of professional indemnity insurance are such that the principles and approach of the contract adjudication technique need little adaptation to achieve full cost-effectiveness, with the broker able to play an important supporting role.

The modifications necessary are only:

1. To the 'feed-in' stage – where modifications will serve to increase the impartiality of the technique.
2. Where the contract adjudication intervention is a very early one and 'preventative' measures can be developed, but impartiality between the parties and their ultimate legal rights must be preserved.

There could be a conflict of interest between the requirements for preserving either the insurers' long-term interest, and the Adjudicator's impartiality as between the parties, i.e. the insured architect (respondent) and the architect's client (generally the claimant) in the dispute between them, and in the situation where the underwriter's interests may be different.

Experienced arbitrators know that many references to them can be disposed of at the preliminary meeting, or a little later, without running the full course of further and better particulars, discovery and hearing, etc. This is particularly the case where an Arbitrator understands more about the problems in the dispute area than the lawyers dealing with the claim and response.

If the testimony of expert witnesses is also freed from the adversarial context of the courts and arbitration room the possibilities of earlier resolution are further enhanced.

Professional indemnity insurance contract adjudication would therefore work as follows and as shown in Fig. 9.2. It would come into operation immediately an insured professional advised his insurance broker or company that there had been an incident or incidents giving rise to the possibility of a claim or that notification of a claim had been made by the professional's client to him.

In suitable cases the broker or insurance company would then advise an Adjudicator that there was the possibility of a claim under a professional indemnity policy. The Adjudicator would then write to both parties to the dispute, or possible dispute, outlining:

1. The Adjudicator's status in the matter;
2. What the Adjudicator knows of the claim;

and would propose an exploratory meeting, which would be without commitment by either party, at which the Adjudicator would take the chair and at which both parties would be represented at the highest possible level. It would be preferable at this stage if the parties' solicitors were not present but if either party wished to be accompanied by their solicitor this would be possible.

The Adjudicator would first request a simple statement of the outline of the claim or claims, not to occupy more than one A4 sheet. On receipt of this statement of claim the Adjudicator would then set out the agenda for the exploratory meeting. This meeting would aim to establish agreement on what the problem was, who were the parties involved, what was the action at issue, and any other key factor.

It may be possible at the end of this exploratory meeting to have arrived at a point of agreement not only on the factors at issue but also on the way to resolve them, or even in some cases, to a resolution of the whole question, in which case the Adjudicator would draw up an 'Award by Consent' and issue this to the parties, and the matter would be at an end for all time with very little cost to anyone.

If not, then the second objective would be for both parties to make a joint appointment of the Adjudicator to resolve the dispute by the subsequent adjudication procedure. After joint appointment, the Adjudicator would reaffirm or establish the terms of reference for the adjudication procedure, and would issue directions as to the subsequent conduct of the reference, including the invitations to any secondary parties to join in the adjudication.

In building disputes it would be necessary for the Adjudicator to have available to him all the necessary expertise and expert evidence on matters where he was not himself qualified and competent but this would be by means of assessors or experts whom the Adjudicator would appoint.

The parties would execute the Adjudicator's directions, including the production of all relevant documents. The Adjudicator would inspect the defects and documents, would hold a Hearing and issue any interim and eventually the Final Award. This would indicate the time by which the Award would need to be rejected by the parties with due notice to the Adjudicator and the other side and indicating their reasons for rejection, otherwise the Award would at the stated time become final and binding upon them.

An insurance underwriter who was indemnifying the professional would therefore have the opportunity, as would the claimant and the insured, to reject the Award within the prescribed period. The underwriter therefore does not risk losing his right to take the matter to the courts but he will know, as will everyone else, the extent of the Award made against him or in his favour and can assess on a commercial basis the cost and risk of going through the courts against the known cost of settlement at that stage.

This would also be subject to the normal 'QC clause', whereby the likelihood of success could be adjudged by Queen's Counsel just as if the matter was an issue between insurance underwriter and the insured he was indemnifying over whether the matter should become a legal action rather than a compromise settlement.

This point would be arrived at much earlier and at much less cost than with the present procedure. If, however, at the end of the exploratory meeting agreement to carry out the adjudication procedure had not been accepted by the parties then the Adjudicator would prepare minutes of the meeting – adding any observations on the position that he considered were appropriate and issue these to both parties, who would then have to proceed with litigation.

Figures 9.3 (a) and (b) show the likely alternative cost profiles for this procedure set against the conventional procedure which it is assessed would save over 60 per cent of the total sums paid out in handling professional indemnity claims. It would also have the following benefits for all parties in professional indemnity disputes:

1. It would deal with the dispute at a very early stage.
2. The claim would be settled much earlier, thus reducing the resources reserved by underwriters.
3. It will resolve the dispute in the area of the technical rather than the legal cause through third-party intervention.
4. It involves only one team of technical and legal experts rather than two or more teams.
5. It would ensure that as far as possible the cost of the dispute itself were related to the amount in question. and
6. In the long term it would provide preventative measures and encourage their use by the parties and so actually reduce the incidence and risk of a dispute arising.

The concept is not one that will eliminate court proceedings entirely although it would reduce substantially the number of cases that do proceed into the courts. It will not entirely eliminate the need for insurers to appoint solicitors whose role in advising on the architect's or engineer's liability will continue where the parties do not adjudicate.

There may also be occasions when insurers need to instruct solicitors to represent the architect's or engineer's interests in adjudication or arbitration proceedings but in a high proportion of cases going to adjudication a legal assessor to assist the Adjudicator is all that will be required and any other expertise necessary can be obtained in a similar way. Thus saving at least half, or probably more, of the costs of the expert and legal views that would otherwise be involved prior to a Hearing.

Finally, where the liability of the insured professional is accepted, the underwriter's loss adjuster can be involved to establish the quantum of a claim and thus the underwriter's liabilities, but once again the procedure would substantially reduce the costs involved.

Figures 9.1(a) and (b) sum up the concept of adjudication in professional indemnity insurance claims. It shows how the 'PICA' procedures pay regard to the factors and the technical functions of the building project through which the dispute has arisen. The PICA Adjudicator examines all the documents, plans, specifications, schedules, etc. (not just the form of contract) and considers the technical customs and practices of the architects, engineers, surveyors and contractors, which are in most cases the real 'stuff' of the dispute.

In short, it considers and resolves the problems in the arena in which they arose rather than in either the environment of the courts and the

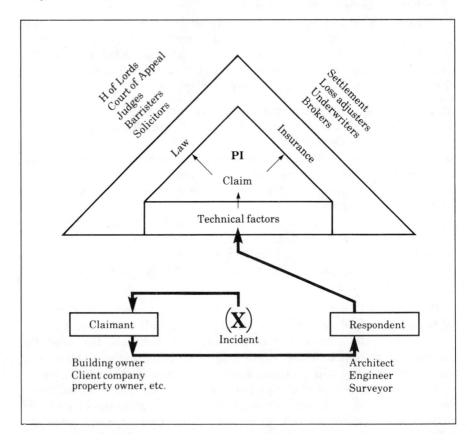

Fig. 9.1 (a) Conventional litigation approach to claim and settlement;

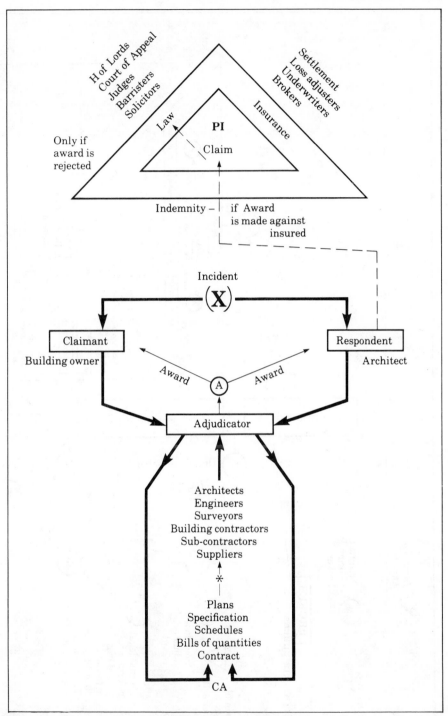

Fig. 9.1 (b) adjudication 'PICA' approach. Alternative path for earlier and more economic dispute resolution.

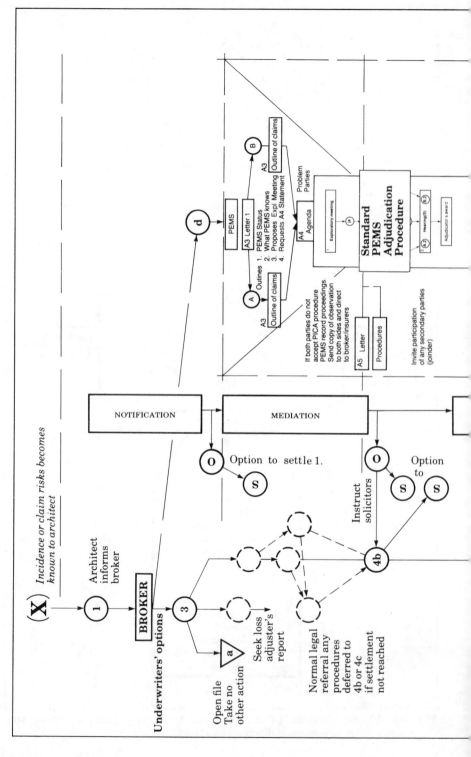

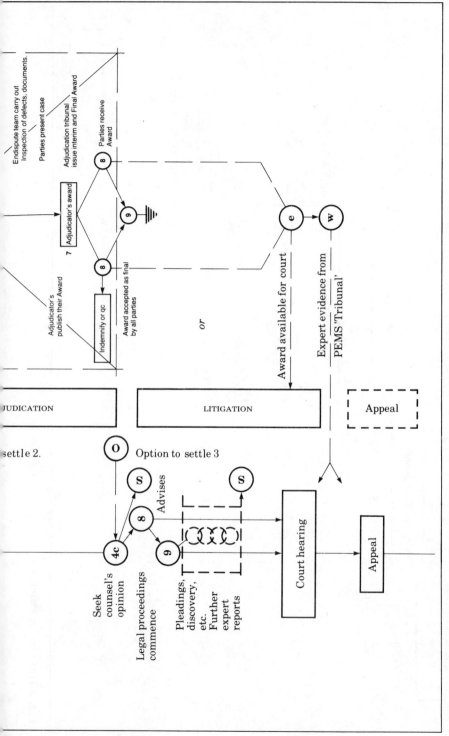

Fig. 9.2 Cost benefits in Professional Indemnity Claims. Underwriter's options to reduce costs and risks.

161

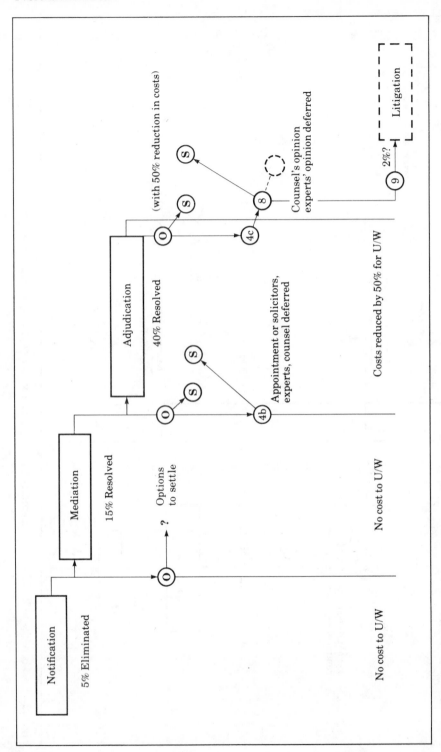

Fig. 9.3 (a)   Underwriters increase opportunity to settle.

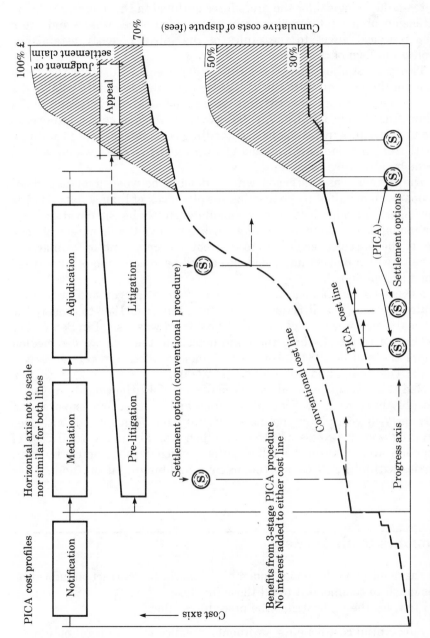

Fig. 9.3 (b) Reduced costs of settlement.

law or the esoteric or commercial arena of the Insurance Industry. It will do this without any risk that the insurers could, if they wish, still reject the Award and proceed as before.

It would be logical for the procedures outlined in this chapter to be an extension of the intermediary role of the insurance broker and could give practical effect to the ethics of the fairly recently established professionalism of the broker.

Two case studies from the author's experience illustrate the economics of the procedure. In the first case where the procedure was used – and so the insurance underwriters were saved all their costs, and in the other (Case Study 1 in Ch. 7, p. 96) where it was not. In the latter case the underwriters incurred dispute-handling costs in excess of £1 million, apart from the damages claimed of £1.6 million – costs which will be borne by all future premiums!

The former was concerned with a dispute between a management company on behalf of its sixteen lessees of a block of luxury flats and the developer. The adjudicators were appointed jointly by the developer and the management company in May 1984 to resolve the disputes between five of the lessees over defects to the roof, balconies and other matters, some of which defects had commenced and been continuous since 1977 when first occupied.

I needed a small measure of support from a lawyer and structural engineer and issued directions during the summer of 1984 to remedy the defects, which were complied with. The Award was issued in September 1984, as a result of which the main defects to the roof were remedied before the end of 1984 – less than 7 months after the reference was made. The total adjudication cost was £3,000.

Had this matter pursued the normal course of litigation there would probably have been six firms of solicitors and at least four experts, and perhaps 2–3 years later the matter would have been settled, with fees totalling well in excess of £15,000, which was about the total cost of remedial works after the adjudication, which was accepted by both parties within the 21 days given, as final and binding upon them.

Benefits to all parties

In the field of professional indemnity insurance contract adjudication has much to commend it to all those involved.

First, for the underwriter the procedures offer:

1. Substantial cost benefits – without prejudice to their legal options;
2. Speed in settlement, thus reducing both the amount reserved against claims; and
3. Substantial interest which those delays occasion.

For the insurance broker, if the adjudication procedures emanate from his involvement, it gives an opportunity to provide a further service between insurer and insured and at a time when both can benefit best from the broker's neutral position.

For the professional, or contractor, as well as for their clients – for whose benefit they have already effected the insurance cover – it provides:

1. A private, prompt and truly impartial analysis; and
2. Speedy adjudication which will not exacerbate the stress and disturbance that such difficulties always produce.

In the long term the procedures, by reducing the cost of handling the dispute, should also lead to lower premiums. Whilst for the claimant it should increase the likelihood of a fuller indemnity payment where he has genuinely suffered damage as a consequence of the negligence of those he employed to protect his interests.

What then stands to be lost, and by whom?

Nothing, it would seem, by the people who are involved in the action for which the insurance is effected. Certainly neither the broker nor the underwriter whose commercial province it is to provide the service and cover, will lose financially, nor will their risks increase.

Constraints on introduction

What then is to prevent the rapid introduction of adjudication techniques into this area and with a highly productive improvement in the current volatile, negative and in every way unsatisfactory situation?

The difficulty beyond just lack of knowledge of the concept and its operation is that the initiative and machinery to bring it about do not lie entirely in any one of the four areas involved.

The broker, the underwriter and the insured are all bound up in their existing and long-established procedures and, unlike large operations all within one corporate control where productivity improves directly from changes made, none are sufficiently involved in the overall process that will be improved to the extent that they can easily see the benefits that would flow from the amended procedures. Further, the resources necessary to implement the concept must essentially lie outside any or all of the principal participants.

But the resources exist and experience is developing in their use of the technique. It now requires a single act of conviction by underwriters to do something differently, or apparently opposite to the norm, before the benefits can flow to all. In this it is perhaps similar to the simple reversal of the joystick operation that was necessary to give back the

165

control of the aircraft to the test pilot when speeds faster than sound were built up. Only then did supersonic flight become possible and now, when required, it is an ordinary and everyday event.

The claimant, the one who stands to gain as much as anyone, will always be outside this particular area, but the insured architect or engineer, his broker and the underwriter will all benefit both financially and in less traumatic activity when claims inevitably arise.

CHAPTER 10

CONCLUSION – TOWARDS MORE EFFECTIVE DISPUTE RESOLUTION

Confliction, says Edward de Bono, is the energy deliberately put into creating conflict, but what is needed is design effort to resolve the dispute and this can only come from third-party intervention.

The Construction Industry, as I have shown, has a built-in potential for conflict arising from the differences always present in values, principles and interests. Thus, when differences arise from unforeseen events, no matter how well the client, design team and contractors have managed the project, better methods of resolving the differences are needed than have hitherto been available.

Sir Hugh Casson, architect and Academician extraordinary, once said of the architect's design task that it was first necessary to analyse all the requirements and elements of the client's need – to make a pile of all the matches – and then set light to them so that in this transmutation something different and exciting emerged in the design that better satisfied the client's requirements.

Dispute resolution by design, or, as I would prefer to call it, by management, from a third party is not providing just a compromise solution with both parties accepting they give up something of their claim, nor a consensus solution where the lowest common denominator prevails. It requires remotivating both sides. They should then accept that a full consideration of **all** relevant issues has been made and that the outcome in the Adjudicator's Award is the same solution they would themselves have arrived at if they had considered the matter before the event, and then struck their bargain!

Where the third-party Adjudicator or Arbitrator has the powers of an *amiable compositeur* this is virtually required of him; but, in my view, proceeding under the 1950 and 1979 Acts and taking **all** matters relevant to the dispute into consideration, the right Arbitrator will arrive at the same conclusions and his Award should therefore follow from his reasoning.

All matters, would mean recognition first of the differing **values** – those of the standards stated by the client, of function, aesthetic, cost and time – as seen from within his own cultural framework, and those presented to the contractors through the skills and labours of the design team. Next, of the conflict in the **design requirements and principles** such as the physical and structural solutions and of economics; and,

167

finally, of **interests** as between the building owner, the design team, the general contractor and the various specialist subcontractors, and all within the context of constraints by planning authorities, by adjoining owners and by the environment generally as expressed in the statutory regulations controlling the project's development. Perhaps it is this latter, legal overlay and the very complexity of modern buildings and the organisations needed to create them that has led to disputes being decided more and more by lawyers and so by the law, an arena far removed from, and virtually irrelevant to, the cause of the dispute.

Is it therefore surprising that few, if any, of those involved in the dispute, save the lawyers who were only involved in the post-cause battle, are satisfied with the outcome!

Managing the dispute, which requires creating, or designing, the environment for, and controlling the procedures to bring about, the resolution of the dispute will be the easier, the closer it reflects the technical, organisational and cultural environment through which it evolved.

Today progress in aircraft design and operation has put world-wide travel within reach of all – and in so doing has also stimulated world trade and increased the potential for dispute across continents and cultures.

The design of modern aircraft illustrates how conflicts in the values required for performance – range, loadings, fuel consumption, safety and comfort conditions for crew and passengers – with the principles for physical structure, aerodynamics and economics and with the conflicts of interest between passengers, operators, manufacturers and the environment have all had to be overcome by the design because in the end the aeroplane must fly, and be acceptable to all its users.

The aircraft design team have had to resolve all these conflicts and make it thus.

With the scale, technology and pace required of modern construction projects it is also unlikely that adjudication by a single mind, albeit that of a technical rather than of a legal judge, will always be satisfactory. A multi-disciplinary tribunal reflecting, but not necessarily mirroring, the skills and technologies involved in the project, will be the structure best fitted to provide the full, fair, swift and economic solution to differences that arise in construction contracts.

Having been at various times client, project manager, designer and responsible for guiding contractors, manufacturers and subcontractors, I have no doubt that every sizeable project should include in the project structure provision for third-party umpiring to be available immediately any matter is called in question. Much as the procedure now recommended by the BPF.

The demands of one-off construction projects pose similar problems to those of aircraft design with conflicts in values, physical principles and human interests throughout their life-cycle. Adjudication, as I have reasoned in this book, is the best way to resolve these conflicts.

Then, when the Award has been made, commercial interests will quickly see how much more acceptable it is to them than any alternative procedure.

The quickest resolution of dispute and the more effective use of human resources, are essential elements in the future progress of modern society. The principles of effective management remain unchanged when applied to the management of dispute, they charge the Adjudicator and Arbitrator with high levels of responsibility for ensuring that the service is made available to the greatest possible extent, at the lowest possible cost and with the least waste of resources.

A concept essentially different from both technology and the law, but owing something to both.

BRITISH PROPERTY FEDERATION
ADJUDICATION PROCEDURES

The BPF produced in November 1973 the report of a working party and a Manual of Procedure for managing building contracts which has become known as 'The BPF System'. Subsequently, with the Association of Consulting Architects they produced the *ACA Form of Building Management 1984*, BPF Edition, which it is intended should be accompanied by a model consultants' agreement based on the forms of the Association of Consulting Engineers.

The system has many innovations stemming from a 'client' orientated study of the building process, and uses 'functional' definitions for the roles of those involved in the design and build process. It uses the titles 'client's representative', 'design team leader', 'design consultant', 'cost consultant' and 'supervisor' (for the works). It also defines excellently in management terminology their roles and responsibilities, authority and accountability.

The biggest innovation is the acceptance of the concept of adjudication 'to solve quickly and simply any disputes which may arise between the client and the design leader (or other consultants), by an independent Adjudicator'. The system also conceives the appointment of an Adjudicator to be appointed at the beginning of the building contract to be available at short notice to provide 'a very quick and simple means of dealing with differences of opinion on matters of valuations, completeness of work and similar technical matters'.

The relevant sections of the System Manual are:

Section 3.8   Disputes and arbitration (during the design phase).
Section 5.10   Disputes and arbitration – procedure: dealing with disputes.

Clause 25   Disputes from *ACA/BPF Form of Building Agreement* are reproduced in full, with the kind permission of both the BPF and the ACA.

3.8 Disputes and arbitration

Selection of Adjudicator

To solve quickly and simply any disputes which may arise between the Client and the Design Leader (or other Consultants), an independent Adjudicator should be appointed at the beginning of Stage 3. He is selected by the Client's Representative with the consent of the Design Leader (and other Consultants). The Adjudicator should be conversant with building development, design procedure, drawing office administration and fees.

Adjudicator's fee

It is recommended that whatever the outcome of a dispute, the cost of the Adjudicator's fee is shared equally between both parties, thus giving a mutual incentive to settle quickly. Moreover, the Adjudicator should be paid on a time basis per dispute, rather than a project fee, which encourages settlement of minor matters without using his services.

Adjudication

In the event of a dispute the Adjudicator carries out an investigation and prepares his decision which is given to both parties. His decision is implemented forthwith. If either party disagrees with the Adjudicator's decision, the matter may be taken to arbitration after practical completion of the project; the Adjudicator's decision shall form part of the evidence to the arbitrator. The Adjudicator should present invoices for his fee to the Client who will recover half the amount from the other party in the dispute.

Should a named Adjudicator be unable or refuse to act, a replacement is appointed with the agreement of both parties. If the parties are unable to agree, either party may ask the President of the Chartered Institute of Arbitrators to appoint a replacement.

5.10 Disputes and arbitration

Appointment of Adjudicator

The object is to resolve disputes quickly and not to let them become prolonged and harmful to cooperation and the project. The BPF System involves the use of an Adjudicator who should be conversant with building costs and methods and with estimating and administration matters. Moreover, he should act as a conciliator wherever possible. He is appointed at the beginning of the contract and is expected to be available at short notice. This provides a very quick and simple means of dealing with differences of opinion on matters of valuations, completeness of work and similar technical matters. The Adjudicator is paid on a time basis per dispute, not a retainer for the whole of the project. His costs are borne equally by the parties to the dispute. Hence there will be an incentive to settle matters without using his services.

If either party is not satisfied with the Adjudicator's decision the dispute may be referred to arbitration after the taking over of the works. The Adjudicator's decision forms part of the evidence to the arbitrator.

Procedure: dealing with disputes

1   The Client's Representative selects an Adjudicator and arranges his fees on a time basis.

2   The proposed Adjudicator is named in the invitation to tender. His name, terms of reference and fees are confirmed after agreement is obtained from the Contractor.

3   If in any case the named Adjudicator cannot or will not act, a replacement is appointed by agreement with the parties in the dispute or, if they cannot agree, by the President of the Chartered Institute of Arbitrators at the request of either party notified to the other.

4   Upon the written request of either party, the Adjudicator promptly investigates the dispute.

5   The Adjudicator records the results of his investigation and gives his decision to both parties.

6   The decision given by the Adjudicator is implemented forthwith.

7   The Adjudicator presents his invoices to the Client, who pays within fourteen days. Half the cost will be recovered from the Contractor through the contract.

Any dispute arising which cannot be resolved by the disputes procedure can be referred to an arbitrator after the taking over of the works.

ACA Form of Building Agreement 1984, BPF Edition

Contents

Guidance notes on the completion of this Agreement are given in italics in the right-hand margin of each page. Clauses or items which may be deleted are shown within square brackets.

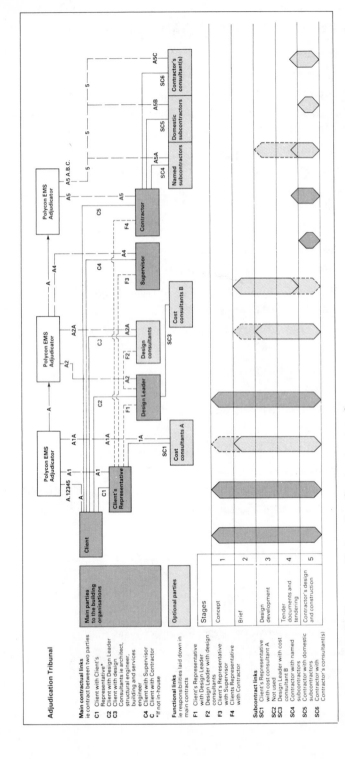

Fig. AI.I I British Property Federation Contract network.

25. DISPUTES

The
Adjudicator

25.1 The term 'the Adjudicator' in this Agreement shall mean

_____ *Insert name*

of

_____ *and address*

or such other person as may be appointed from time to time under Clause 25.4 to act as Adjudicator in place of the Adjudicator so ap- pointed. The Adjudicator may from time to time, by notice to the Employer, the Client's Representative and the Contractor, delegate the performance of his duties as Adjudicator under this Agreement to a person to be named by him in such notice. The person so named shall have authority to perform the duties of the Adjudicator under this Agreement until such time as the Adjudicator shall notify the Em- ployer, the Client's Representative and the Contractor from time to time that such person's authority is terminated. Any decision of the person so named within the period of his authority shall, for the purposes of this Agreement, be treated as a decision of the Adjudicator.

Matters refer-
able to the
Adjudicator

25.2 Save in respect of the matters referred to in Clause 1.4 Alternative 1 (if applicable), if any dispute or difference of any kind whatsoever shall arise between the Employer or the Client's Representative and the Contractor at any time prior to the Taking-Over of the Works arising out of or in connection with this Agreement or the construction of the Works (either during the progress or after the completion or abandon- ment of the Works) as to:-

(a) any adjustment or alteration of the Contract Sum; or

(b) the Contractor's entitlement to and the length of any extension of time for the taking-over of the Works or any Section under Clause 11.5; or

(c) whether the Works are being executed in accordance with the Contract Documents; or

(d) either party's entitlement to terminate the Contractor's employ- ment under Clause 20.1 or 20.2; or

(e) the reasonableness of any objection by the Contractor under Recital E to this Agreement or under Clauses 4.1 or 10.2;

then such dispute or difference shall in the first place be referred to and settled by the Adjudicator who, within a period of 5 working days after being requested by either party to do so, shall give written notice of his decision to the Employer, the Client's Represen- tative and the Contractor. In giving his decision, the Adjudicator shall, without prejudice to the generality of his powers, be entitled to adjust the dates for the taking-over of the Works or of any Section previously stated, adjusted or fixed and/or award such damage, loss and/or expense to the Contractor or to the Employer as shall, in his opinion, be fair and reasonable in respect of the dispute or difference referred to him or caused by the reference to him and the Contract Sum shall be adjusted accordingly. The Adjudicator shall have power to request either party to provide him with such oral or written statements, documents or infor- mation as the Adjudicator may determine but not so as to delay the giving of written notice of his decision in accordance with this Clause 25.2

Effect of
Adjudicator's
decision

25.3 In giving a decision under Clause 25.2, the Adjudicator *shall be deemed to be acting as expert* and not as arbitrator and his decision under Clause 25.2 shall be final and binding upon the parties until the Taking-Over of the Works and shall forthwith be given effect to by the Contractor and by the Employer and the Contractor shall proceed with the Works with all due diligence whether or not either party requires arbitration as provided in Clause 25.5. Such reference to the Adjudicator shall not relieve either party from any liability for the due and punctual performance of such party's obligations under this Agreement.

Appointment of another Adjudicator   **25.4**   If the Adjudicator (whether the person named in Clause 25.1 or any other person to whom such person has delegated the performance of his duties as Adjudicator pursuant to Clause 25.1) fails to give his decision in accordance with the provisions of Clause 25.2 or if he shall be unable or refuse to act, all disputes or differences under Clause 25.2 shall be referred to and settled by a person to be agreed between the parties or, failing agreement within [5] working days after either party has given to the other a written request to concur in the appointment of an Adjudicator, a person to be appointed upon the application of either party by the President or a Vice-President for the time being of the Chartered Institute of Arbitrators to act as Adjudicator for all the purposes of this Agreement.

Arbitration on Adjudicator's decision   **25.5**   If the Adjudicator appointed under Clause 25.4 of this Agreement refuses or neglects to give a decision or if, upon receipt of the Adjudicator's notice of his decision under Clause 25.2, either party is dissatisfied with the same such party may, subject to the provisions of Clauses 20.1 and 20.2, within [20] working days after receiving the Adjudicator's notice of his decision or after the expiry of the time within which it should have been given, give notice to the other requiring that the matter should be referred to the arbitration of a person to be appointed under Clause 25.6. If no claim to arbitration has been notified by either party to the other within [20] working days as aforesaid, such decision shall remain final and binding upon the parties.   *

* *number must same as 25.5 above*

Arbitration   **25.6**   All disputes or differences in respect of which a decision (if any) of the Adjudicator has not become final and binding under Clause 25.5 and save in respect of the matters referred to in Clause 1.4 Alternative 1 (if applicable), all disputes or differences arising out of or in connection with this Agreement or the carrying out of the Works as to any matter or thing of whatsoever nature (including any matter or thing left to the discretion of the Client's Representative or to the withholding by the Client's Representative of any certificate to which the Contractor may claim to be entitled or any issue as to whether or not any certificate is in accordance with the provisions of this Agreement) which are not referable to the Adjudicator under Clause 25.2 shall, unless the parties agree to the contrary, be referred to the arbitration and final decision of a person to be agreed between the parties, or, failing agreement within [10] working days after either party has given to the other a written request to concur in the appointment of an arbitrator, a person to be appointed on the request of either party by the President or Vice-President for the time being of the Chartered Institute of Arbitrators. Such reference shall not be opened until after the Taking-Over or alleged Taking-Over of the Works or termination or alleged termination of the Contractor's employment except with the written consent of the Employer and the Contractor: Provided always that if, in the Employer's opinion, any dispute or difference to be referred to arbitration under this Agreement raises matters which are connected with matters raised in another dispute between the Contractor and any of his sub-contractors or suppliers and provided that such other dispute has not already been referred to an arbitrator, the Employer and the Contractor agree that such other dispute shall be referred to the arbitrator appointed under this Agreement and such arbitrator shall have power to deal with both such disputes as he thinks most just and convenient.   *

Arbitrator's *powers*	**25.7**	The Arbitrator appointed under Clause 25.6 shall (save as aforesaid) have full power to open up review and revise any decision, opinion, direction, certificate or valuation of the Client's Representative or of the Adjudicator and the award of such arbitrator shall be final and binding on the parties. No decision given by the Adjudicator under this Agreement shall disqualify him from being called as a witness and giving evidence before the Arbitrator on any matter whatsoever.

ALTERNATIVE 1

Law of this *Agreement*	**25.8**	The law of England shall be the proper law of this Agreement and the provisions of the Arbitration Acts 1950 to 1979 or any statutory modification or re-enactment thereof shall apply to any arbitration under this Agreement and such arbitration shall take place in England.	*Delete if the law* *of Scotland* *applies*

ALTERNATIVE 2

Law of this *Agreement*	**25.8**	The law of Scotland shall be the proper law of this Agreement and the provisions of the Arbitration (Scotland) Act, 1894 or any statutory modification or re-enactment thereof shall apply to any arbitration under this Agreement and such arbitration shall take place in Scotland.	*Delete if the law* *of England* *applies*
		The parties hereby agree that the procedures contained in Administration of Justice (Scotland) Act, 1972 Section 3 shall not apply to any arbitration under this Agreement.	*Delate if case* *stated procedure* *to apply*

POLYCON ENDISPUTE MANAGEMENT SERVICES ADJUDICATION PROCEDURES

Polycon Endispute Management Services Ltd was formed by a number of senior members of the Chartered Institute of Arbitrators to provide the essential resources that were seen to be needed to deal with the concept of adjudication during the progress of large or complex construction and other contracts.

Polycon adjudication procedures include provision for the resolution of non-contractual disputes, that is to say those where tortious liability is involved, which they classify as **dispute adjudication**.

For contractual disputes where there is already an arbitration clause, or where the parties wish to enter into adjudication after the dispute has arisen and so avoid reference to formal arbitration, they have a procedure called **contract adjudication**, and thirdly there is a full procedure of **contract management adjudication**, which is for use throughout the period of a contract and can be entered into after the main contract has been signed and before a dispute has arisen, or alternatively, when a difference has occurred or looks likely to occur. This procedure, developed before the BPF manual and system were published but has many similar aspects, although it goes further in making directly available to the parties practical measures for both prevention and cure.

There follows extracts from the procedures developed by Polycon Endispute Management Services Ltd relating to the appointment procedures and conduct of adjudication:

1. 'CA' Appointment form and operation flow diagram
2. 'DA' Appointment form and operation flow diagram
3. 'CMA' Appointment form
4. 'CMA' Application
5. 'CMA' Operational procedures and flow diagram

Polycon Endispute Management Services Limited

APPOINTMENT AS:-

CONTRACT ADJUDICATOR

WHEREAS

A.   A contract was entered into for the execution of work at ....

....

between ....

of ....

and ....

of ....

and B.   That contract contained a Clause whereby in the event of a dispute arising either party could make application for the dispute to be resolved by Arbitration in accordance with the Arbitration Acts 1950 and 1979 and any subsequent enactments.

C.   A dispute has arisen out of or connected with that contract.

D.   Both parties wish to submit that dispute to Adjudication prior to taking any legal action.

NOW THEREFORE PRIOR TO ANY OTHER ACTION

1.   We hereby refer the matters listed as in dispute between us to the assessment and adjudication of a Polycon Endispute Adjudicator appropriate to this dispute.

2.   As a condition of this Appointment we jointly and severally agree as follows:-

   i)   to pay the fees and expenses in relation to this Appointment in accordance with the schedule attached:

   ii)   to provide adequate security for the due payment of the fees and expenses and any award connected with this appointment should the Adjudicator so require:

   iii) to abide by and comply with the directions of the Adjudicator until the Award is published.

   iv)   to notify the other party(ies) to this agreement and the Adjudicator within 14 days of the publication of the Adjudication in the event that we are not prepared to accept it as final and binding and so wish to reserve our rights to seek Arbitration or Litigation at a later date in accordance with the terms of

         the contract dated ....../....../......

   v)   that in the event that the Adjudication referred to in iv) above is not accepted by us as final and binding we hereby agree to its submission as evidence in relation to this dispute in any subsequent action brought by either party should either party wish to do so.

Signed: .... 1st Disputant

Signed: .... 2nd Disputant

CA(OD).1
7/85

Fig. A II.1 (a)

Appendix II

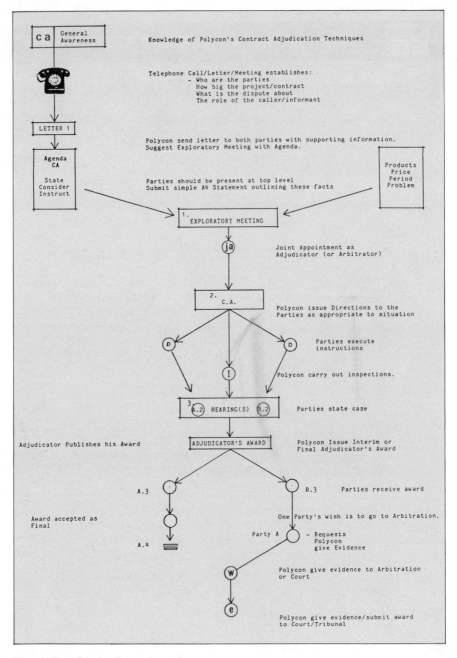

Fig. A II.1 (b) CA Procedure flow.

180

Polycon Endispute Management Services Limited

APPOINTMENT AS:-

DISPUTE ADJUDICATOR

WHEREAS

A. A contract was entered into for the purpose of ....

....

between ....

of ....

and ....

of ....

and B. A dispute has arisen between the parties.

and C. The parties seek an Adjudicator's appraisal to prevent further proceedings either by litigation or arbitration and to appoint Polycon Endispute Management Services Ltd. to make such appraisal.

NOW THEREFORE PRIOR TO ANY OTHER ACTION

1. We hereby refer the matters listed as in dispute between us to the assessment and adjudication of a Polycon Endispute Adjudicator appropriate to this dispute.

2. As a condition of this Appointment we jointly and severally agree as follows:-

   i)   to pay the fees and expenses in relation to this Appointment in accordance with the schedule attached:

   ii) to provide adequate security for the due payment of the fees and expenses and any award connected with this appointment should the Adjudicator so require:

   iii) to abide by and comply with the directions of the Adjudicator until the Award is published.

   iv) to notify the other party(ies) to this agreement and the Adjudicator within 14 days of the publication of the Adjudication in the event that we are not prepared to accept it as final and binding and so wish to reserve our rights to seek Arbitration or Litigation at a later date in accordance with the terms of

        the contract dated ....../....../......

   v)   that in the event that the Adjudication referred to in iv) above is not accepted by us as final and binding we hereby agree to its submission as evidence in relation to this dispute in any subsequent action brought by either party should either party wish to do so.

Signed: .... 1st Disputant

Signed: .... 2nd Disputant

DA(OD).1
7/85

Fig. A II.2 (a)

181

Appendix II

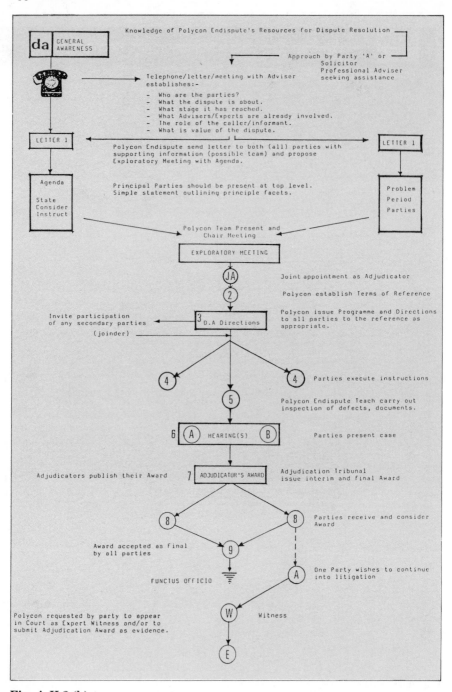

Fig. A II.2 (b)

182

Polycon Endispute Management Services Limited

APPOINTMENT AS CONTRACT MANAGEMENT ADJUDICATORS

WHEREAS

1. On the . . . . day of . . . . 19 . . .

    a contract was entered into for the purpose of . . . .

    . . . .

    between . . . .

    of . . . .

    and . . . .

    of . . . .

and 2. The parties require the services of Polycon Endispute Management Services Ltd. to adjudicate
    during the course of this contract in the event of a dispute arising.

and 3. That in the event of such dispute arising both parties to the contract undertake to:-

    i)   abide by and comply with the rulings of the Adjudicator throughout the period of the
         contract;

    ii) to pay the costs of the adjudication service or to ensure that it is paid by the party whom
         the Adjudicator assesses should meet the fees;

    iii) to give notice within the prescribed period after each adjudication and at the end of the
         contract if they intend not to accept the Adjudication as final and binding upon them in all
         respects.

    iv) that in the event of any matter related to or arising out of the main contract which shall
         become the subject of litigation or arbitration after the completion of the contract to the
         submission of the adjudication awards as evidence in such action;

4. That this appointment shall be irrevocable by either of us without the written consent of the
    other prior to the completion of the project which is the subject of the contract.

5. That the appointment of PEMS as Adjudicator will commence on signing and will continue until
    completion of the contract and/or the payment of the final account, whichever be the sooner.

Signed by the Parties:-

Signed: . . . . Party A

Signed: . . . . Party B

Date: . . . .

MA(OD)1

Fig. A II.3 (a)

Appendix II

CMA SCHEDULE OF FEES AND EXPENSES

1. **Appointment Fee**

   The fee, payable jointly by the parties upon Polycon taking up and confirming the

   the appointment will be £ . . . . (. . . . .

   . . . .)

   This fee will cover the initial appraisal and the six month period commencing on:-

   . . . . / . . . . / . . . .   and shall include for:-

   i) the inspection and perusal of the contract documents and its organisation and
   informing the parties of their observations on these by Polycon Endispute;

   ii) the notification to the parties by the Adjudicators and to any participating
   sub-contractors of the invocation rules through which Polycon Endispute's link
   adjudicator may be requested to provide adjudication services during the progress
   of the works or course of the contract.

2. **Retaining Fee**

   After the first six months have expired Polycon shall be paid a fee as a retainer for
   each subsequent 6 month period the sum in of £. . . . . to provide immediate
   response to a request of invocation to provide their adjudication services.

3. **Time Based Fees for Adjudication**

   The fee for a Contract Adjudication Service will be calculated from the time of
   invocation on a time basis for all time spent on the reference as follows:-

   i) Time spent at meetings and hearings - £ . . . . . . per day.

   ii) Time spent on the case outside of meetings and hearings, including any time spent
   travelling - £ . . . . per hour.

   iii) These time based fees will be assessed on completion of each particular
   adjudication, which will also allocate the responsibility for the payment of these
   time based charges between the parties.

   iv) Payment for the adjudication shall be made by the parties responsible within 14
   days of the invoice date.

4. **Expenses**

   Specific outgoing expenses incurred in connection with the appointment for travel,
   subsistance, hire of rooms, postages, telephone, telex, cable, copying, recording and
   transcribing services, reports of any experts and advisers or researchers whose
   services have been agreed with the parties and any other items will be charged at net
   cost.

5. Value Added Tax will be added where appropriate.

Fig. A II.3 (b)

184

APPLICATION

CONTRACT MANAGEMENT ADJUDICATION

is a management technique which benefits all the

parties to a multi-faceted project.

* **For the Employer/Building Owner**

  it prevents hold-ups that might otherwise delay
  completion and reduces the financial risks of
  long drawn out claims which otherwise lack a
  determination. It should also result in keener
  tendering as the risk element to the Contractor
  of delayed decisions is reduced.

* **For the Architect/Engineer/Consultant**

  it eliminates the difficulty of being sole judge
  in his own cause and the conflict of interest
  between his own position and that of his Client
  when the Contractor makes claims where there is
  doubt on either responsibility or quantum. It
  also provides the professional team with the
  opportunity for consultation prior to making a
  decision on contentious matters which might
  otherwise be challenged later and so also reduces
  his professional risks.

* **For the Contractor**

  impartial technical judgement with experience of
  all aspects of the construction operation ensures
  a rapid and fair hearing with speedy resolution
  of claims which might otherwise be unresolved
  until long after the work has been practically
  completed.

* **For the Sub-Contractor**

  (Provided he too has accepted the provision
  within his Contract)
  it ensures that his interests are kept in proper
  balance vis-a-vis both the main Contractor and
  the Employer and eliminates the problems of
  conflict between himself and other contractors or
  suppliers.

* **For All Involved**

  it provides an economic framework that helps to
  ensure that interests which may conflict as the
  contract progresses are held in balance and
  quickly resolved by disinterested experts whose
  participation is limited to only those matters
  where the parties and their professional advisers
  or managers cannot agree. Thus keeping up the
  momentum of the project towards the common
  objective of early and profitable completion.

Fig. A II.4 (a)

POST TENDER ACTION PRIOR TO WORK COMMENCING ON SITE

When both parties have signed the Adjudication Appointment Form:-

* The Adjudicator will acknowledge and accept the appointment;

* Polycon Endispute Management Services Ltd. will render an Invoice for one half of the Appointment Fee to both parties for payment within fourteen days;

* Polycon Endispute will then nominate a "Link-man" to whom the responsibility for monitoring the Contract will be delegated.

* The "Link-man" will then call for:-

    i) The Contract Documents;

    ii) The Employer's and the Contractor's Project Organisation; and

    iii) The Project Programme (network, Gant Chart, or other Planning Data.

Appraisal

* The Polycon Endispute Management Services' Adjudicator will then study these documents, consulting with other PEMS specialists if necessary, and then issue to both parties to the main contract:-

    i) The rules for invoking the services of the Adjudicator in the event of a difference arising during the progress of the Works;

    ii) A Schedule of those to whom the Rules should be circulated;

    iii) Any observations he may have on gaps or overlaps in the documents or project organisation.

Monitor Mode

* The "Link-man" will ensure the rules and observations have been received and understood and then will await notice of any dispute requiring Adjudication.

Fig. A II.4 (b)

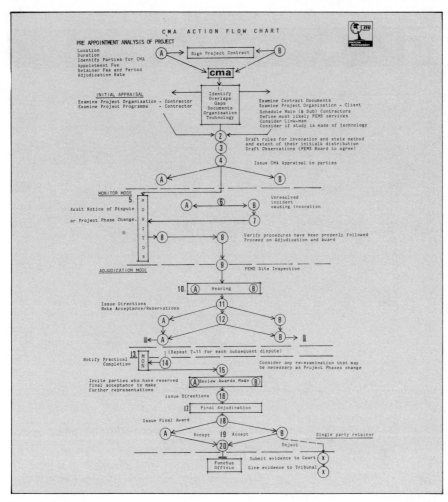

Fig. A II.5 (a)

Polycon Endispute Management Services Limited

C.M.A. ACTIVITY SCHEDULE

PRELIMINARY

A. The appointment of PEMS as Contract Management Adjudicator can be made at any time after the project contract has been made between the parties. It may also be signed after an incident has already ocurred causing a dispute during the continuation of the contract.

B. As a first step in either situation the CMA appointment form must first be signed by both parties - then the operations will be carried out by PEMS through a Link-man who will be delegated with the authority as Adjudicator and/or Chairman of Tribunal of other PEMS specialists whose experience may be required by the subject-areas of any dispute.

INITIAL APPRAISAL

1. A Link-man will be appointed by PEMS's Board and notified to the parties. The Link-man will then seek or receive from the parties the main project contract documents, the project organisation documents, if any, that apply to both client and the main contractor's organisation, the project programme or network, a schedule of the main and sub-contractors already nominated and involved. The Link-man Adjudicator will examine these documents to identify gaps and overlaps in:-
   a) the contract documents;   b) the contract organisation;
   and also consider whether any study should be made of the contract technology.

2. The Link-man/Adjudicator will then consider whether any other PEMS member should be nominated to the project tribunal and whether anyone else should also study the contract documents.

3. He will then draft the invocation rules and state method and extent of the initial distribution of these rules. He will also consider whether any other Contractors or Sub-contractors, Agents, etc. should be covered by the Rules for CMA Procedure. He will draft his observations, submit and agree these and the Invocation Rules with PEMS Board.

4. PEMS will issue the CMA appraisal and Invocation Rules to the parties.

MONITOR MODE

5. The Link-man will ensure that the parties have received and understood the rules for invocation and will then await notice of any dispute.

6. Upon the incidence of any matter causing a dispute to arise either party invokes the procedure rules and gives notice of a dispute requiring Adjudication.

8. The Link-man verifies that the invocation procedures have been properly followed and then arranges to carry out an appropriate investigation/site inspection.

ADJUDICATION

9. The Link-man visits site (accompanied other Adjudicator or Specialist?).

10. Link-man/Tribunal holds meeting(s) on site and hears representations from all parties involved.

11. The Link-man issues Directions and any interim award to both parties.

12. The Link-man notes acceptance of his Award or any reservations of the parties.

13. Return to Monitor Mode to await further incidents, notification of change of main contract phases, or Practical Completion.

14. The parties notify Practical Completion of the contract and indicate whether they consider a further Adjudication or final award is required.

15. Link-man and/or Tribunal reviews interim awards, and if necessary:-

16. Issues directions for any final hearing prior to considering and drafting Final Award.

17. Link-man/Tribunal drafts final Adjudication Award and submits to PEMS Executive Board - Any dissentions or minority opinions are considered and award published.

18. Company Secretary ensures all fees are collected and issues final award to parties.

19. Company Secretary monitors acceptance (functus officio), or:

20. Company Secretary receives notification of rejection by one party and advises Link-man, checks that all fees have been received.

X.1 Company Secretary awaits request by any party for copies of award or attendance of Link-man or others to give evidence.

X.2 Company Secretary keeps Adjudicator/Witness informed of dates of Court/Arbitration hearing.

CMA(OD)3.iv

Fig. A II.5 (b)

CONTRACT MANAGEMENT ADJUDICATION

RULES OF PROCEDURE to apply to Joint Adjudication Services

1. On Appointment

The Adjudicators will be supplied by the parties with copies of the contract documents and with details of the organisation and management structure, responsibilities and procedures applicable to the contract and project, within fourteen days of appointment.

2. The Adjudicators will then, following a perusal of these documents and an examination of the details and within fourteen days of their receiving these details, prepare and submit to the parties the procedures that are to be applied in the event of a dispute arising during the course of the contract as a result of which any one party wishes to invoke the adjudication procedure and obtain a Contract Management Adjudication from Polycon Endispute.

3. With this submission Polycon Endispute will nominate a "Link-man" who will have familiarised himself with the general nature of the work to be carried out under the contract so as to be able to respond immediately in the event of his services or those of other Polycon Adjudicators being invoked by the parties.

Polycon Endispute will also supply the parties with their observations on the contract documents and organisation proposed for the project and highlight any area where they have noted matters that might lead to dispute if not given appropriate further attention by those responsible.

This initial consideration will be covered by the appointment fee providing it does not require more than 10 man-days of Adjudicator's time.

4. Monitoring Service

Having made their observations on the contract documents to the parties the Adjudicators will throughout their period of retention be available to commence an investigation and to adjudicate immediately any party instigates the invocation procedure.

5. Adjudication

If any party invokes an Adjudication the Link-man will then:-

i)   first ensure that the other party or parties have been informed in writing of his investigation;

ii) commence his investigation within 7 days involving such other Polycon resources as required.

iii) whilst making his investigation the Adjudicator will not be bound by the strict rules of evidence although he will conduct himself judicially and in accordance with natural justice. For example he will not only look at evidence presented but may also search for all existing evidence.

iv) If any party submits written material to him it will be copied to the other parties involved if it has not already been so distributed and they will be given appropriate time by the Adjudicator to submit a written response, should they wish to do so.

v)   The adjudicator will, if he considers it necessary, visit the site or premises giving notice to the parties of his intention to do so so that they may if they wish be represented whilst the Adjudicator makes his inspections, and records by photographic or other means the situation as he finds it;

vi) The Adjudicator shall make all investigations he considers desirable, or is reasonably asked to make by the parties, and shall talk to whomsoever he wishes in connection with the dispute, including the Engineer or other consultants who have been involved in the preparation of the Contract Documents or design of the project.

vii) When he has formed his opinion on the matters submitted to him for adjudication he will call the parties' representatives before him - on the site or elsewhere as is appropriate - and inform them of his views. He will then give each party the opportunity to address him verbally, the party who has invoked the procedure having the right to elect to speak first, or last.

viii) The Adjudicator will then, normally within 48 hours, prepare his written Adjudication and, if appropriate, issue directions on the action to be taken thereafter, together with his reasons therefore and submit these to the parties.

ix) As part of his written adjudication he will deal also with the costs of this Adjudication and allocate these between the parties, and order when and how and by whom these shall be paid.

Fig. A II.6 (a)

General Conditions as Procedures after Adjudication Invoked

6. The parties are irrevocably bound to uphold, and carry out forthwith, the instructions and directions given by the Adjudicator throughout the period to practical/substantial completion of the contract. After the issue of any and each Adjudication the parties will notify each other and the Adjudicator within 21 days of its publication if they do not accept the Adjudicator's Award as final and binding upon them. Such notice shall include a statement of the reasons for their non-acceptance of its finality. Upon the practical/substantial completion of the contract the parties shall notify the Adjudicator and at the same time indicate whether they require the Adjudicator to issue a further consolidating Award.

   The Adjudicator will, upon notification of the practical completion of the contract, review all the awards made and, if necessary, notify the parties and give any further Directions necessary for the submission of further representations or the holding of further hearings prior to any final Adjudication and the publication of a final Adjudication Award.

   Upon the publication of this final Award the parties shall have 28 days or such other longer period as the Adjudicator shall consider reasonable in all the circumstances in which to notify one another and the Adjudicator of their rejection of this Award as final and binding. Such notification shall include a full statement of their reasons for rejection. Without a notification to the contrary the Adjudication shall become final and binding upon the parties.

7. The time spent on any reference after the Adjudicator has established the correct invocation procedures have been observed( )shall be paid for on the hourly and daily rates set out in Clause 3 of CMA Appointment Schedule. In making the Award as a result of the Adjudication the Adjudicator will indicate in the Award how and by whom these costs shall be paid.

   The Engineer, Architect, or any other Consultant who has been concerned with the preparation of the contract documents and who is named therein or in the Adjudication instructions given under Rule 5 above shall be entitled to confer with the Adjudicator as to the proper interpretation or course of action under the contract and to state that he has done so in any instructions he issues under the contract.

   Time spent by the Adjudicator on such consultations shall be taken as part of the Adjudicator's engagement and the Adjudicator will indicate in writing how and by whom these additional costs shall be paid as if it had been invoked as for a dispute as in Rule 5 viii).

8. In the event that a notice is given reserving their rights to refer the matters to arbitration or litigation at the end of the contract either party may submit the evidence recorded by the Adjudicator and his written Adjudication to the Arbitration Tribunal and may call him before the tribunal to further explain his reasoning.

9. Special conditions relating to (Specific Project) . . . .

   . . . .

   1. Will indicate Times and Durations for Action;

   2. Identify - people and posts embraced by procedures;

   3. Indicate Locations for Notices, Events, etc.

Fig. A II.6 (b)

INDEX